中国的节日与民俗

CHINESE TRADITIONS AND FESTIVALS

修订版
Revised Edition

祝　健　薛丽卿　吴文彬　著
Jian Zhu　Regina Hsueh　Wen-Bin Wu

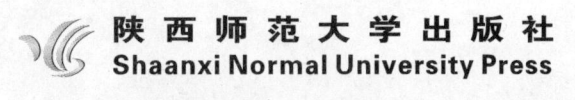

陕西师范大学出版社
Shaanxi Normal University Press

图书代号:ZH8N0067

图书在版编目(CIP)数据

中国的节日与民俗/祝健编著. – 西安:陕西师范大学出版社,2003.2
ISBN 978 – 7 – 5613 – 2414 – 1

Ⅰ. 中… Ⅱ. 祝… Ⅲ. ①节日 – 中国 – 对外汉语教学 – 语言读物 ②风俗习惯 – 中国 – 对外汉语教学 – 语言读物 Ⅳ. H195.5

中国版本图书馆 CIP 数据核字(2003)第 003122 号

中国的节日与民俗

祝健 薛丽卿 吴文彬 著

责 任 人	王 岚
封面设计	徐 明
出版发行	陕西师范大学出版社
社　　址	西安市陕西师大 120 信箱(邮政编码:710062)
网　　址	http://www.snupg.com
经　　销	新华书店
印　　刷	陕西金德佳印务有限公司
开　　本	787mm×1092mm　1/16
印　　张	13.75
字　　数	173 千
版　　次	2008 年 3 月第 2 版
印　　次	2008 年 3 月第 1 次印刷
书　　号	ISBN 978 – 7 – 5613 – 2414 – 1
印　　数	1 – 2000 册
定　　价	32.00 元

读者购书、书店添货或发现印刷装订问题,请与营销中心联系、调换。
电　　话:(029)85251046(传真)　85233753　85307864
E – mail:snupg@126.com

CONTENTS

Chapter 1	Spring Festival — Red Envelopes and the New Year's Eve Meal	1
Chapter 2	The Lantern Festival — Viewing Lanterns and Eating Sweet Dumplings	10
Chapter 3	Marriage — the Matchmaker and the Wedding Banquet	19
Chapter 4	Drinking Wine and Drinking Tea	27
Chapter 5	Tomb Sweeping Day —the Day for Commemorating One's Ancestors	35
Chapter 6	Stuffing Dumplings — Inviting Guests to a Lively Feast	42
Chapter 7	Three Generations under One Roof	48
Chapter 8	The Water Splashing Festival — a Folk Custom from the Southwest	54
Chapter 9	Education in Ancient Times	61
Chapter 10	The Dragon Boat Festival — Dragon Boats and Zongzi	68
Chapter 11	Old Customs —the Lying-In Period after Childbirth and Foot Binding	74
Chapter 12	Mid-Autumn Festival — Moon Viewing and Moon Cakes	80
Chapter 13	Birthday Banquet and the Newborn's Name	86
Chapter 14	The Double Ninth Festival	91
Chapter 15	The Story of Chinese Characters	97
ENGLISH TRANSLATION OF THE STORIES		103
CHINESE CHARACTERS IN "CHINESE MADE EASIER" 6-60		161
CHINESE CHARACTERS		181
CHINESE-ENGLISH VOCABULARY LIST		197

目 录

1. 春节——红包和年夜饭　　　　　　　　　　1
2. 元宵节——看灯笼和吃元宵　　　　　　　10
3. 结婚——红娘和喜酒　　　　　　　　　　19
4. 喝酒和喝茶　　　　　　　　　　　　　　27
5. 清明节——纪念亲人的日子　　　　　　　35
6. 包饺子——热热闹闹地请客　　　　　　　42
7. 三代同堂　　　　　　　　　　　　　　　48
8. 泼水节——西南民俗　　　　　　　　　　54
9. 古时候的教育　　　　　　　　　　　　　61
10. 端午节——龙舟和粽子　　　　　　　　　68
11. 古老的习俗——坐月子和小脚女人　　　74
12. 中秋节——赏月和月饼　　　　　　　　　80
13. 生日饭和新生儿的名字　　　　　　　　86
14. 重阳节　　　　　　　　　　　　　　　　91
15. 汉字的故事　　　　　　　　　　　　　　97

ENGLISH TRANSLATION OF THE STORIES　　103

实用速成汉语 6-60　汉字　　　　　　　　161

CHINESE CHARACTERS　　　　　　　　　　181

CHINESE-ENGLISH VOCABULARY LIST　　　197

PARTS OF SPEECH

Nouns / Pronouns	名词 / 代词	N / PN
Measures	量词	M
Numbers	数词	NU
Specifiers	特指词	SP
Action Verbs	动词	V
Equative Verbs	同位动词	EV
Question Words	疑问词	QW
Auxiliary Verbs	助动词	AV
Adjectives	形容词	SV
Adverbs	副词	A
Particles	语助词	P
Time Words	时间词	TW
Prepositions	介词	CV
Moveable Adverbs	可移副词	MA
Conjunctions	连接词	Con
Verb-Object	动宾复合词	VO
Place Words	地方词	PW
Bound Forms	限制词	BF
Resultative Verb	结果动词	RV
Expressions	惯用词	EX/PH

第一章　春节——红包和年夜饭

春节是中国最重要的节日。为什么叫春节呢？"春节"的意思就是冬天快要过去，春天就要来了。也就是说一年快要过去，新的一年就要开始了。一年过了一年，所以过春节又叫"过年"。

每一个中国人都会告诉你，过年是很重要的。每年的这个时候，一家人都会高高兴兴地聚在一起。过完年以后，人人都希望有一个又好又新的开始。

为了迎接新的一年，春节快要来的时候，每家每户都很忙。第一件大事，就是把房子收拾干净。家里的每一个地方都必须打扫得十分干净，家里的每一个人也要收拾收拾自己的东西，所以大人们忙，小孩子们也忙。春节前的那几天，不管男人还是女人，大家都忙着为新年做准备，有的打扫屋子，有的整理院子，每一家都是这么忙。干干净净过春节是大家都喜欢的，不是吗？

春节前，每家还有另外一件大事要忙：就是买过年的东西。过年要用的东西很多，吃的菜、穿的衣服、鞭炮、点心、酒，等等，这些都是春节要用的东西。买这些东西是很重要的，因为过春节的时候，差不多所有的人都在家里休息，差不多所有的商店也都不开门，所以你必须买很多的东西来准备才行。

家里收拾干净了，过年的东西买好了，这时大家就忙着准备过春节：男人们忙着写春联；女人们忙着做年夜饭；老人们忙着准备新衣服；小孩子们忙着准备要玩的鞭炮。春联就是两张长长的红纸，在上面写上祝福新年的话。中国人最喜欢红颜色，所以在红纸上写上美好的话，那就更好了。写完以后，就把春联贴在大门的两边，所以过年的时候，家家户户的大门口都可以看到红红的春联，非常好看。

有的时候，中国人把"福"字写在一张红纸上，然后把它贴在大门上面。不过他们常常把"福"字故意倒过来贴，不知道的人就会说："福倒了！福倒了！"听起来，就好像是在说："福到了！福到了！"每家每户听到这样的话，就更高兴了！

中国人把春节的前一天叫做"年三十"，把年三十晚上叫"除夕"。年三十的早上，女人们都起得很早，准备晚上的"年夜饭"，因为除夕是春节最重要的时候。古时候，中国的交通很不方便，如果有人在离家很远的地方读书或做生意，回家是一件很不容易的事情。但是不管路有多远，年三十晚上，在外地的人都得放下所有的事情，回到家和家人一起吃年夜饭，因为在中国人心里，家是最重要的地方。

从前,"年夜饭"是一年里最重要的一顿饭,也许也是一年中最好的一顿饭。因为那个时候,中国人的生活条件不是很好,很多家庭只有在过年的时候才能吃上鸡鸭鱼肉。现在,中国人的生活好多了,人们可以经常吃到很多好吃的东西,但是年夜饭仍然是一年里最重要的一顿饭。因为回到自己的家,又见到了自己的家人,大家在一起一边吃年夜饭,一边有说有笑,就会把过去一年中所有的辛苦和不高兴的事情全部忘记。所以说,吃年夜饭是中国人一年中最高兴的事情了。

年三十晚上还有很多别的开心的事情。吃过了年夜饭,小孩子们就等着大人们给红包。"红包"就是一个红色的纸包,人们把钱装在里面,作为送给亲戚朋友的礼物。小孩子们向大人们说一些新年里好听的话,大人们就把红包送给他们,"新年好"是大人们最喜欢听到的祝福的话。一年里,小孩子们最喜欢这个时候了,因为他们拿到了红包,就可以去买自己喜欢的东西了,比如说鞭炮、玩具。

年三十的晚上,虽然每个人都有点累,但是大家都不想休息,都要等到晚上十二点,等着新年的到来。十二点一到,每家都同时开始放鞭炮,新的一年来到了,每个人又长大了一岁!

第二天,也就是新年的第一天,每个人都穿上新衣服。新年里看见别人的第一句话就是:"过年好!"每个人都希望有一个很好的开始。大人们带着小孩子去看亲戚朋友,虽然小孩子们不一定想去，但是他们知道如果去的话，就可能会得到红包，这是他们所希望的。

　　春节很快就高高兴兴地过去了，人们又开始了自己原来的生活，工作的人又要开始工作，读书的人也要开始读书了。春节是一个新的开始，大家都希望今年比去年更好，大人们都希望新的一年能挣到更多的钱，当然，很多小孩子也希望明年的春节会收到更多的红包！

问题

1. 春节的前几天为什么要收拾很多东西呢？
2. 春节的前一天叫做什么？
3. 中国人为什么要把"福"字倒过来贴呢？
4. 年夜饭为什么很重要？吃年夜饭时什么才是最令人高兴的？
5. 猜猜看，为什么春联是红色的，红包也是红色的？
6. 年三十晚上，大家都做些什么事呢？
7. 新年的第一天，大人小孩都做些什么事呢？
8. 小孩子们希望去看家人和朋友吗？为什么？

The English translation of the stories starts on page 103

生 词

* = new character only (i.e. it did not appear in Chinese Made Easier lessons 6-60)
A list of the characters in Chinese Made Easier lessons 6-60 is on p.161-180.

*	章	zhāng		chapter
1.	红包	hóngbāo	(N)	a red envelope containing money (as a gift or bribe)
2.	年夜饭	niányèfàn	(N)	dinner for the whole family on the eve of Chinese New Year
*	夜	yè		night, dark
*	冬	dōng		winter
*	聚	jù		to assemble, gather (together); to come or put together
*	希	xī		hope, desire, long for; strange
*	望	wàng		hope, expect; to view, watch
3.	迎接	yíngjiē	(V)	to receive; to greet, welcome
*	迎	yíng		to receive; to greet, welcome
*	接	jiē		to receive, accept; to welcome; to join, connect
*	户	hù		household, family; a door
*	把	bǎ		a handle/hold; to watch over
4.	收拾	shōushi	(V)	to tidy up, put (things) in order

Chapter 1: Spring Festival

*	收	shōu		to gather, collect; to retrieve; to accept, receive
*	拾	shí		to pick up, collect; 10 (official)
*	净	jìng		clean, pure; to cleanse, purify; empty, vain
*	须	xū		to have to, must, to need; necessary, proper; a beard
*	扫	sǎo / sào		to sweep, clear away; wipe out, weed out, exterminate / broom
5.	十分	shífēn	(A)	100%, very, completely
*	管	guǎn		to take heed to; to manage, control; a tube or pipe
*	屋	wū		room; house
*	整	zhěng		whole, entire; exactly; orderly, neat; to tidy, set in order
*	理	lǐ		reason, cause; law, principle
6.	鞭炮	biānpào	(N)	string of firecrackers (放 = to let off)
*	鞭	biān		to whip, flog; firecrackers
*	炮	pào		a cannon, big gun
*	酒	jiǔ		wine, liquor, alcoholic drink
7.	春联	chūnlián	(N)	New Year couplets (written on strips of red paper and pasted on doors)

*	联	lián		to unite, to connect, to join; allied (forces), joint (efforts)
8.	祝福	zhùfú	(N)	a blessing
	祝(福)	zhù(fú)	(V)	to wish (as a blessing)
*	祝	zhù		to wish happiness; celebrate; to congratulate
*	福	fú		happiness, blessing, bliss
*	颜	yán		dyes, colors; features, face; reputation
9.	美好	měihǎo	(SV)	(of abstract things) happy, bright, fine
*	贴	tiē		to paste on; to subsidize; appropriate
10.	家家户户	jiājiāhùhù	(N)	every family and household
*	它	tā		it (neuter gender)
11.	故意	gùyì	(A)	intentionally, on purpose
*	故	gù		cause, reason; incident, event; former, previous
12*	倒	dào	(V)	to invert, place upside down; on the contrary; to pour
*	倒	dǎo		to collapse, be overthrown; to topple, fall over/down
13.	除夕	chúxī	(N)	Lunar New Year's Eve
*	夕	xī		dusk, evening; slanting, oblique

14.*	古	gǔ	(SV)	ancient, antiquated
*	交	jiāo		to intersect; to exchange; to hand in/over (to)
*	通	tōng		to communicate; to lead to; to flow unobstructed
*	读	dú		to study; to read
15.	外地	wàidì	(PW)	other parts of the country (i.e. other than where one is now)
16.	从前	cóngqián	(A)	formerly, in the past, a long time ago
*	顿	dùn		Measure for a meal; to pause
17.	条件	tiáojiàn	(N)	conditions; terms (of an agreement)
*	庭	tíng		a hall or yard; court of justice
*	鸭	yā		duck
18.	仍然	réngrán	(A)	still, yet
*	仍	réng		still, yet
*	笑	xiào		to laugh, smile; to ridicule, deride
*	辛	xīn		hard, toilsome; bitter, acrid
*	苦	kǔ		bitter; miserable, difficult
*	全	quán		whole, complete; perfect; absolute(ly)
*	忘	wàng		to forget; to neglect, overlook

*	装	zhuāng		to install, pack, load; to store, to keep; to pretend; to feign
*	戚	qī		relatives by marriage
*	物	wù		thing, matter; the physical world
19.	比如（说）	bǐrú (shuō)	(EX)	for example
20.	同时	tóngshí	(A)	at the same time, simultaneously
*	同	tóng		same, identical; together; equal; to agree
*	岁	suì		a year; age (of a person)
*	句	jù		a sentence
*	原	yuán		origin, source, beginning
*	挣	zhèng		to earn (money / a living)
21.	令人	lìng rén	(VO)	to make one (e.g. sad, angry)
*	令	lìng		to cause something to happen; a directive, an order
*	猜	cāi		to guess; to suspect

NOTES

一家人 = the whole family

到来 = the arrival of ..., the coming of ...

第二章　元宵节——看灯笼和吃元宵

农历新年后的第十五天是"元宵节",也是新的一年中第一个大的节日。每年的这一天,天上的月亮又大又圆,这是新年里的第一次月圆。虽然这个时候很多地方天气还很冷,可是每个人的心里还是很暖和的,因为看见天上美丽的月亮,每个人都很高兴。

从春节到元宵节,一共十五天,这些天都是在过年。元宵节以后,新年的热闹才慢慢过去,所以元宵节也是春节的最后一天。这一天,很多地方还是很热闹:有的地方唱歌,有的地方跳舞,还有的地方有许多有意思的活动。大家都像过年一样的高兴,玩得很开心,一直到了晚上,还是想继续玩下去。

在古时候,人们晚上出门是不太容易的,因为那个时候没有电灯。太阳一下山,每个人都回到自己的家里,一般晚上也不出门,如果有人晚上没有回家,家里的人都会不太放心。但是,元宵节是春节的最后一天,所以每个人都希望能出去走走。

传说，古时候有一个皇帝，他觉得元宵节是个特别的节日。他想这天晚上的月亮是这么明亮和美丽，如果大家都能出来走一走、看一看，不是一件很好的事情吗？所以皇帝就让他的国民这天晚上都出来玩。从那个时候起，每年元宵节的晚上，大家就都到外面去玩了。

虽然元宵节晚上的月亮很明亮，可是外面还是比较黑。为了让大家都能看得清楚，每家房子的前面都挂起了灯笼。尤其是一些有钱的人家，他们挂上很多大灯笼，把晚上照得像白天一样亮。很多人走在路上，手里也提着灯笼。就这样，天上有很大的月亮，地上有很多的灯笼。每个人都喜欢在这个晚上出来玩，因为到处都有灯笼，所以元宵节又叫做"灯节"。

元宵节的晚上，大家都会去寺庙前面看灯笼。那里会有很多各种各样的灯笼，这些灯笼都挂在寺庙前面。所有的灯笼都是大家用手做出来的，有大的，有小的，看上去非常漂亮。古时候的灯笼都是用纸做的，纸上常常画着很多漂亮的图画，看着这些美丽的灯笼，每个人的眼睛都是明亮的。

为了让元宵节更热闹，寺庙前面常常还会有一些活动——唱歌、跳舞等等。元宵节还有一个特别的活动：人们会问一些有趣的问题，让别人来猜。如果有人猜对了，就送给这个人一件礼物，因为他猜对了问题。所以，问问题的人很高兴，猜对问题的人也很高兴，看热闹的人们也都一起高兴。

很多时候，这些问题都写在灯笼上，大家看灯笼的时候，同时就可以看问题，猜问题。这是只有元宵节才有的活动，我们把它叫做"猜灯谜"。

比方说，以前有这样一个题目：有一个东西生出来的时候是四只脚，长大以后变成了两只脚，老了以后变成了三只脚。猜一猜这是什么？这就是人。因为人刚刚生出来的时候，是用手和脚在地上爬的；长大以后，就用两只脚走路了；到老的时候，需要用东西来帮助他走路，所以看起来就像是三只脚。你猜对了吗？元宵节的时候，常常有人会问很多这样有趣的问题。

元宵节的时候，大人和小孩都会出来玩。大人喜欢一边看灯一边和别人聊天。很多小孩子拿着自己做的灯笼，高兴地跑来跑去，从很远的地方看，他们提的灯笼就像一条条活的小金龙，一会儿飞到这里，一会儿飞到那里，真是有趣！

很多没结婚的年轻男女，也会在这个时候出来玩，每个人都穿着漂亮的衣服，大家一起去看灯笼，趁这个机会也可以认识很多朋友。不过，中国古时候常常都是男人和男人在一起，女人和女人在一起，男人和女人不能走得太近，这是当时的文化。

除了看月亮和看灯笼，这一天每家每户都要吃元宵。元宵是一种圆圆白白的东西，就像天上圆圆的月亮一样。在中国，北方人和南方人做的元宵是不一样的。但是，有一点是一样的，吃元宵就是希望每个人在新的一年都过得好，也希望全家人都能经常在一起。

元宵节高高兴兴地过去了，新的一年又开始了。为了美好的生活，每个人都应该好好地工作。工作的人准备出去工作，做生意的人开始准备做生意，学生们也开始准备上学念书了。春风轻轻地吹来，花也慢慢地开了，从现在开始，每个人又都要忙起来了！

问题

1. 元宵节和春节有什么不同？
2. 元宵节有些什么活动？
3. 古时候，为什么人们一般晚上不出来？
4. 元宵节为什么又叫做灯节？
5. 元宵节时，哪些地方有灯笼？
6. 元宵节时，大人和小孩都在做什么？
7. 平时，年轻男女为什么不可以在一起玩？
8. 有一种水果，外面黄里面白，看起来像月亮。你猜是什么水果？
9. 元宵节要吃什么东西？元宵是什么样子的？
10. 元宵节过后，大家要做什么？

生 词

	宵	xiāo		night, dark, evening
1.	灯笼	dēnglong	(N)	a lantern
	灯节	dēngjié	(N)	Lantern Festival
*	灯	dēng		lamp, light, lantern
*	笼	lóng		a bamboo cage, basket; to include, to encompass
2.	农历	nónglì	(N)	the lunar calendar
*	农	nóng		farming, agricultural
*	历	lì		to pass through, to undergo, to experience; an era, an age
3.	天上	tiānshang	(PW)	in the heavens/skies
	地上	dìshang	(PW)	on the ground
*	圆	yuán		round (in shape), circular; complete; satisfactory
4.	月圆	yuèyuán	(N)	full moon
*	冷	lěng		cold (lit. & fig.)
*	暖	nuǎn		warm
*	丽	lì		beautiful, fine, elegant
*	闹	nào		to disturb, to agitate; noisy; experience (natural disasters)
*	唱	chàng		to sing; to chant

*	歌	gē		a song; to sing, chant, praise
*	跳	tiào		to jump, leap; throb, pulsate; to skip over, omit
*	舞	wǔ		to dance; to brandish; to stir up, agitate
*	直	zhí		straight; direct; continuous; outspoken, frank
*	继	jì		to continue, carry on; to inherit, succeed to
*	续	xù		to continue, renew, extend
*	阳	yáng		sun, solar; male, masculine; positive (electricity, etc.)
5.	下山	xià-shān	(VO)	(of the sun) to set [also: to descend a mountain]
*	般	bān		kind (of), sort (of), class (of)
6.	传说	chuánshuō	(V) (N)	rumour has it; people say that… legends, hearsay
*	传	chuán zhuàn		to propagate, pass on, spread biography
7.	皇帝	huángdì	(N)	emperor
*	皇	huáng		imperial, royal; term of respect for an ancestor
*	帝	dì		imperial; emperor, ruler; a god or deified being
*	特	tè		special, unique, unusual
8.	明亮	míngliàng	(SV)	bright, well illuminated

Chapter 2: The Lantern Festival

9.	国民	guómín	(N)	citizen, the people
*	民	mín		the people (as opposed to the government)
*	让	ràng		to let; to permit, allow; by; to give way, yield, concede
*	黑	hēi		dark; black (color); evil, sinister
*	挂	guà		to hang (up), to suspend; to worry, to be anxious; to register (at hospital or P.O.)
*	尤	yóu		especially; mistake, error; feel bitter against
*	其	qí		this, that, the; he, she, it, they
10.	人家	rénjiā	(N)	a home, residence; other people
11.	照	zhào	(V)	to shine upon, illuminate
*	手	shǒu		hand; a skilled person
12*	提	tí	(V)	to carry (by hand); to mention; to raise, to lift by hand; to obtain, make delivery
*	处	chù		a place/location; a department
		chǔ		to be faced with; to deal with
*	寺	sì		temple, monastery, mosque
*	庙	miào		temple, shrine
13.	各种各样	gèzhǒnggèyàng		each & every kind of ...
*	各	gè		each, every; all

第二章　元宵节　17

14. 看上	kànshàng	(RV)	to take a fancy to (CME L.52 1.3)
* 画	huà		paint/draw / painting/drawing; to plan, to design; to mark off
15. 图画	túhuà	(N)	picture, drawing
16* 图	tú	(N)	picture, chart, diagram, map; to scheme, conspire, plan
* 眼	yǎn		the eye; tiny hole or opening
* 睛	jīng		the eye-ball, the pupil of the eye
* 谜	mí		riddle, conundrum, puzzle
17. 题目	tímù	(N)	topic, subject (of a speech or article) [also: a question or problem (in an exam)]
* 目	mù		the eye; to look, to see; division, category
* 脚	jiǎo		foot; leg or base (of something)
* 变	biàn		to change, alter; uncommon; accident, tragedy
* 成	chéng		to become; achieve, accomplish; 10%; acceptable, all right
18* 爬	pá	(V)	to crawl, creep, lie face down; to climb, to clamber
* 助	zhù		to assist, to help, to aid
* 聊	liáo		to chat
19. 金龙	jīnlóng	(N)	golden dragon
* 金	jīn		gold; metal; money, wealth

*	龙	lóng		dragon; imperial, of the emperor
*	轻	qīng		light (in weight); simple, easy; mild, gentle
*	趁	chèn		to take advantage of (an opportunity)
20.	文化	wénhuà	(N)	culture, civilization
*	化	huà		to convert, transform, change; chemistry
21.	上学	shàng-xué	(VO)	to go to school
22*	吹	chuī	(V)	to blow, puff; to brag, boast
*	平	píng		equality; level, even; peaceful

PATTERN

一会儿…… 一会儿……　　one moment doing this, one moment doing that

第三章　结婚——红娘和喜酒

如果一个男人爱一个女人，同时这个女人也爱那个男人，他们可以结婚吗？在古时候的中国，这是不容易的，很多时候也是不可以的。因为那时候，一个人的婚姻常常是要由父母来决定的。从小到大，一个女孩子是不能随便出门的，所以女孩子认识男孩子的机会不多。十六岁以后，他们的父母就会开始为他们找对象。有的时候一个孩子还没有出生，父母就已经决定这个孩子以后应该和谁结婚了。

以前，结婚最重要的条件是社会地位。每个人都希望找和自己社会地位一样的人结婚，有钱人找有钱人结婚，没有钱的人找没有钱的人结婚。因为他们相信，社会地位一样的人，结婚后才会很幸福。但是怎么才能找到和自己社会地位一样的人呢？很多时候，这些事情都需要一个人的帮助，这个人就是"红娘"。

在中国，红娘经常是一个已经结了婚的女人，她认识的人很多。如果有人想要结婚，就请红娘帮忙。红娘的工作就是介绍一个男人和一个女人认识，帮助他们结婚。

结婚以前，两个人都不认识，怎样让这两个不认识的人结婚呢？这个时候，就需要红娘出来帮双方说好话。

开始的时候，男方的家人会请红娘到女方的家里去，看看女方和她的家人，问问女方是不是想和男方结婚。红娘有的时候问男方家人的意见，有的时候又帮女方的家人出主意，所以为了能让他们两个人结婚，每天都很忙。她最希望的就是两个人能结婚，如果结了婚，双方的家人都会很感谢她。红娘不只是一个工作，也是在为别人做好事呢！

如果女方的家人答应结婚，红娘就会有很多事情要做，并且还要注意很多事情，这样，结婚的时候才不会出什么问题。开始的时候，男方的家人会请红娘送一些礼物到女方的家里：如果女方的家人收下了这些礼物，结婚就"应该"没有问题了；如果女方的家人没有收下礼物，结婚的事情可能还有一些问题。

然后，男方的家人会到女方的家里去。这一次是男方真正提出结婚的事情，男方会送给女方钱和非常好的礼物。如果女方收了，结婚的事就定了。男方回家以后，就要决定结婚的日期和请客的事情。男方和女方都希望结婚的日子快一点到来。对男女双方和他们的家人来说，结婚是一件很大的喜事，所以结婚的那一天是很热闹的。结婚的男的叫新郎，结婚的女的叫新娘。这一天，新郎要带一些人去接新娘，把新娘从她家接到自己的家里。新娘穿着最漂亮的红衣服，她的心情是又高兴又难过：高兴是因为自己要结婚了；难过是因为要离开自己的父母了。所以结婚的那一天，新娘会哭也会笑，大家都知道新娘的心情，也就不觉得很奇怪了。

新郎和新娘结婚的时候，很多人都会来看新娘。在这一天，新娘是最漂亮的人了，可是太多的人来看新娘，她会很不好意思。古时候新娘的头上都会盖一块红布，不让别人看到她的脸。虽然看不见新娘的脸，可是看到新娘，大家还是很高兴。

这个时候，每个人都必须注意很多事情：不可以随便说不好的话、不客气的话，也不可以做大家觉得不好的事情。这个时候做事情，最好问问知道的人，像母亲、奶奶或者红娘，因为她们都是很有经验的人，有什么问题，大家都会问问她们的意见。

结婚的两家都会请亲戚朋友来喝喜酒。喝喜酒就是请大家吃饭，这个时候，你可以吃到最好的菜，喝到最好的酒。大家高高兴兴地在一起，说说笑笑，两家人也多了一次认识的机会。大家和新郎新娘一起喝酒，希望新郎新娘能永远在一起，也希望他们快一点生小孩，生很多很多的孩子，因为中国人认为孩子多是一件非常好、非常有福的事情。

到了晚上，新郎还在外面和很多人喝酒，这时候，新娘已经回到了房间里等新郎，但是新娘头上的红布要等新郎来拿下来。喝完喜酒以后，很多朋友会去新郎新娘的房间，用很多方法和新郎新娘开玩笑，要他们两个人做很多奇怪的事情，或者问他们一些奇怪的问题。开了许多玩笑以后，朋友们才会离开。中国人把这种风俗叫做"闹洞房"。

　　结婚的这一天可能是新郎新娘见面的第一天。新郎轻轻地拿下新娘头上的红布，新娘很不好意思地低下头来，不管新郎新娘长什么样，现在他们已经是夫妻了。结婚以后，丈夫就要好好地工作，妻子也要好好地做家里的事。一天又一天，两个人才开始真正认识对方，真正地去爱对方。

问题

1. 古时候的中国，婚姻是由谁来决定的？
2. 古时候的中国，为什么有钱人要和有钱人结婚，没钱的人会和没钱的人结婚？
3. 红娘的工作是什么？
4. 为什么新娘会哭也会笑呢？
5. 为什么新娘的头上有一块红布？
6. 新郎什么时候才能看到新娘的脸？
7. 你喜欢中国古时候先结婚后相爱的方式吗？

生 词

1.	红娘	hóngniáng	(N)	matchmaker, marriage go-between (or 媒人 méiren)
*	娘	niáng		mother; girls or women (collectively)
2.	喜酒	xǐjiǔ	(N)	wedding feast
*	爱	ài		love, affection; be fond (of)
3.	婚姻	hūnyīn	(N)	marriage
*	姻	yīn		(relations through) marriage
*	由	yóu		by, up to (someone); from; reason, cause, source
*	决	jué		to decide; certain, sure
*	随	suí		to submit to; to accompany; to follow on after
4.	对象	duìxiàng	(N)	(marriage) partner, boy/girl friend [also: (e.g. sales) target group]
*	象	xiàng		a portrait; elephant, ivory; a phenomenon
*	社	shè		society, community, organization
5.	地位	dìwèi	(N)	social position or standing (of a person)
6.	幸福	xìngfú	(SV/N)	blissful / happiness & well-being

24　Chapter 3：Marriage

	有福（气）	yǒu fú(qi)	(SV)	blessed, favored by fortune
*	幸	xìng		well-being, happy;　luckily
*	介	jiè		to lie between;　upright
*	绍	shào		bring together, join;　continue
7.	双方	shuāng fāng	(N)	both parties, both sides (in a dispute or agreement)
*	双	shuāng		a pair (of), a couple (of);　both
8.	好话	hǎohuà	(N)	a good word, word of praise
9.	男方	nánfāng	(N)	the bridegroom's family, the man's side
10.	女方	nǔfāng	(N)	the bride's family, the woman's side
11.	出主意	chū zhǔyi	(VO)	to provide an idea, give advice
*	主	zhǔ		lord, master, chief;　officiate at
*	感	gǎn		to feel, perceive; feeling, emotion; to affect, to be moved
*	答	dā / dá		to answer, reply;　reciprocate
*	并	bìng		and, also;　even, equal with
*	注	zhù		to direct one's attention or gaze; to pour (liquids)
12.	出问题	chū wèntí	(VO)	to incur problems
13.	收下	shōuxià	(RV)	to accept, receive

14.	真正(的)	zhēnzhèng(de)	(A)	actual, real;　actually, really; genuine
15.	喜事	xǐshì	(N)	a happy occasion (e.g. wedding)
16.	新郎	xīnláng	(N)	bridegroom
*	郎	láng		husband, man;　master
17.	新娘	xīnniáng	(N)	bride
18.	心情	xīnqíng	(N)	mood　(lit.: heart-feelings)
*	哭	kū		to cry, weep, wail
*	奇	qí		strange, uncanny;　wonderful
*	怪	guài		strange, queer;　ghost, monster; to blame
*	盖	gài		to cover; a lid or covering; to build, construct;　affix (a seal)
19*	布	bù	(N)	cloth, textiles　(M: 块　piece of)
*	脸	liǎn		face　(lit. & fig.)
*	者	zhě		(particle used to form adverbials)
*	验	yàn		to test, examine;　verify, prove
20.	永远	yǒngyuǎn	(A)	eternally, forever
*	永	yǒng		eternal, everlasting, permanent
*	俗	sú		customs (of a people); common, ordinary;　vulgar, unrefined
21.	闹洞房	nào dòngfáng	(VO)	to disturb the bridal chamber

*	洞	dòng		a cave, a hole; to see, penetrate
*	低	dī		to lower; low
22.	夫妻	fūqī	(N)	married couple; husband & wife
*	夫	fū		man, adult, male, master
*	妻	qī		wife
*	丈	zhàng		an elder, a senior
23.	对方	duìfāng	(N)	the opposite party, the other side (e.g. in a dispute)
24.	相爱	xiāng'ài	(V)	to love one another
25.	方式	fāngshì	(N)	approach, method
*	式	shì		model, style, mode, pattern

第四章　喝酒和喝茶

中国人平常吃的东西，主要都是面食和米饭，除了这些以外，青菜、水果和肉也都很重要。但是，中国人的生活中还有两样东西是不能少的，如果没有这两样东西，生活就会变得很没有意思了。那么，这两样东西是什么呢？就是酒和茶。

酒和茶在中国人的社会生活中是很重要的。很多时候人们都会用到它们：有的时候，人们拿酒和茶来纪念去世的亲人；喝喜酒的时候，大家也会用酒和茶来恭喜新郎新娘；有朋友来拜访的时候，人们更喜欢用酒和茶来招待朋友。有了酒和茶，生活就变得更热闹、更有趣了。

中国人喝酒有很长的历史了。三四千年以前，中国人就知道怎么做酒，从那个时候开始，中国人就喜欢喝酒了。人们常常在休息的时候，喝一点酒，聊聊天、说说笑话。喝了酒以后，每个人的脸都是红红的，心里也觉得热热的，大家一高兴，就把心事都说出来了，这样，大家也就变成了好朋友。

从古到今，许多有名的人都爱喝酒。历史上有一个很有名的诗人，叫<u>李白</u>，他很喜欢喝酒。每次喝了酒，他的诗就会写得更好。听说他常常端着酒杯，对着月亮，请月亮一起喝酒。你看，古时候的诗人是多么特别啊！李白就是这样写出了许多很好的诗。不过，传说李白因为喝了太多的酒，后来掉到水里死了。

中国的酒有很多种，每个地方做出来的酒都不一样，喝酒的习惯也不一样。北方的人比较大方，喝酒的时候都是大口大口地喝，因为他们觉得这样喝酒才有意思。而南方的人比较细心，喝酒的时候都是小口小口地喝，因为他们觉得慢慢喝酒才有意思。可是不管怎么喝，反正最后酒都喝到肚子里去了。

不但南北方喝酒的习惯不同，而且每个人喝酒的习惯也不一样，喝酒时的心情也有很大的不同。有的人高兴的时候，就要找人一起喝酒，让别人知道他很高兴；有的人难过的时候，也会找人一起喝酒，让朋友知道他很难过；还有的人没有什么事，也会找人一起喝酒，让大家都知道他没事情做了。就这样，你找我喝酒，我找你喝酒，想要喝酒的时候，是不难找到理由的。但是我们都知道，喝酒太多对身体不好。

在中国，喝茶也是很受欢迎的。很久以前，中国人就开始喝茶了，那么，喝茶是怎么开始的呢？有一种说法是，古时候有一个人正在烧水，有几片树叶落到了开水里。很快，开水变了颜色，黄黄的，还有一点香味。因为这种水是用树叶做的，所以人们就把它叫做茶。开始的时候，大家把茶当作一种药，后来因为茶真的太好喝了，所以大家在不生病的时候，也喜欢喝它了。现在，有很多人差不多每天都要喝茶。

茶有很多种，红茶、绿茶、茉莉花茶……在这些茶里，有冬天长的茶和夏天长的茶。不同的茶，因为生长的时间不一样，喝起来就会觉得不一样。在中国，喝茶是一门很大的学问，很多人都研究喝茶的方法，所以在古时候，有不少人写过关于茶的书，里面写了很多关于茶的事情。可见，茶在中国是很重要的。

中国人喝茶，一般都是在心情好、要休息的时候，因为只有注意喝茶的时间和方法，茶才会好喝。不管是北方人还是南方人，大家都是慢慢地喝茶，而且在喝茶的时候，大家也常常喜欢吃一些好吃的点心。喝喝茶，吃吃点心，和自己的好朋友在一起聊聊天，真是比做什么都快乐！

喝太多的酒不好，但是，喝茶也有一些事情需要注意。第一，放了很久的茶最好不要喝。这种茶我们叫老茶，它会变得很苦，而且对身体不好。第二，茶不能和药一起吃，因为茶本来就是一种药，它会让别的药发生变化，变得没有作用，所以，吃药的时候喝茶，药就对你没有什么帮助了。第三，茶和酒一样可以经常喝，但是不要喝得太多。如果喝太多的茶，你可能就不想吃饭了。

喝酒和喝茶其实不只是让自己觉得很舒服，它们最大的好处还是能让我们常常和朋友在一起。喝酒或者喝茶的时候，朋友和朋友的感情会变得更好。本来两个不认识的人，如果在一起喝酒、喝茶，一边聊天，一边就慢慢地认识了对方。所以，如果你有机会去拜访中国朋友，带一些好酒或者好茶给他，他一定会很高兴。

问题

1. 生活里，少了哪两种东西就会觉得很没有意思？
2. 中国人什么时候会用到茶和酒？
3. 喝酒的时候会做些什么事呢？
4. 诗人李白喝了酒，会做些什么事呢？
5. 北方人和南方人喝酒的习惯有什么不同？
6. 中国人什么时候会喝酒？
7. 传说茶是怎么来的？
8. 喝茶时，要注意哪些事情？
9. 喝茶和喝酒最大的好处是什么？

生 词

1. 主要(的) zhǔyào(de) (SV) major, essential, chief
2. 面食 miànshí (N) wheat foods (e.g. noodles)
* 食 shí food; to eat
3. 纪念 jìniàn (V/N) to commemorate / remembrance
* 纪 jì an historical record, annals; age (of a person); a century
* 世 shì world; generation
4. 亲人 qīnrén (N) close relatives (i.e. parents, children, brothers & sisters)
* 恭 gōng respectful, reverent
5. 拜访 bàifǎng (V) to visit, pay a call on
* 访 fǎng to visit, call on; inquire about
* 招 zhāo to beckon (with one's hand); to recruit, enlist; to attract
* 待 dài to treat (someone); await for
  待 dāi to stay (at a place) [呆]; later on
* 史 shǐ history, chronicles, annals
6. 心事 xīnshì (N) matters/worries on one's mind
7. 诗人 shīrén (N) poet
* 诗 shī poem; poetry

*	端	duān		to carry gingerly; an extreme; correct, proper, upright; a beginning
8.	酒杯	jiǔ bēi	(N)	wine glass, wine cup
9.	对着	duìzhe	(V)	facing (an object or person)
10.	多么	duōme	(A)	How ...! What a ...!
*	啊	a		(exclamatory particle)
*	掉	diào		to drop, fall; to turn, move
*	死	sǐ		to die; extremely (= RVE)
11.	大方	dàfang	(SV)	generous & liberal
12.	口	kǒu	(M)	mouthful
13.	而	ér	(Con)	but, and yet, nevertheless
14.	细心	xìxīn	(SV)	careful, think of all aspects
*	细	xì		detailed; thin, slender; fine, intricate; tiny, small
15.	慢慢来	mànmanlái	(PH)	to take one's time, not rush
*	反	fǎn		reverse, opposite; to turn back
*	肚	dù		stomach, abdomen, bowels
16.	理由	lǐyóu	(N)	reasons, grounds, explanations
*	身	shēn		the body; in person, oneself
*	体	tǐ		the body; shape, form
17.	受欢迎	shòu huānyíng	(VO)	to be well-received/liked

*	受	shòu		to receive, accept; to endure, suffer
18.	说法	shuōfǎ	(N)	a way of reasoning; line of argument or interpretation
19.	烧	shāo	(V)	to boil, cook, roast, burn
20.	树叶	shùyè	(N)	tree leaf, foliage (M: 片)
	叶子	yèzi	(N)	leaf
*	树	shù		tree; to erect, establish
*	叶	yè		leaf, petal
21.*	落	luò	(V)	to fall, descend; decline, wither
22.	香味(儿)	xiāngwèi(r)	(N)	fragrant smell; aromatic flavor
*	味	wèi		flavor, taste, smell, odor
*	药	yào		medicine, medicinal drugs
*	绿	lǜ		green (color)
23.	茉莉花	mòlìhuā	(N)	white jasmine (flower)
*	茉	mò		white jasmine
*	莉	lì		white jasmine
*	夏	xià		summer; a Chinese dynasty
24.	生长	shēngzhǎng	(V/N)	to grow, to develop / growth
25.	门	mén	(M)	(Measure for courses/subjects)
26.	学问	xuéwen	(N)	erudition, learning, scholarship

*	研	yán		to investigate, to research
*	究	jiū		to examine, investigate; finally
*	于	yú		then, than; in, on, at, by, from
27.	可见	kějiàn		it's obvious/perceived that
28.	作用	zuòyòng	(N)	(e.g. drugs) effect; (e.g. machinery) uses, functions
*	实	shí		real, true; practical; tangible
29.	感情	gǎnqíng	(N)	emotional feelings, devotion (between friends & relatives)

第五章　清明节——纪念亲人的日子

大家都知道，一年有春、夏、秋、冬四个季节。但是，在古时候，中国人除了把一年分成四季，还把它分成了二十四个节气。这样，每一个月就都有两个节气。节气可以帮助古时候的人，特别是农民可以更好地注意天气的变化。清明节这个节气也是个节日，如果用西方的方法计算，大概就是每年的四月五日前后。

清明节是中国所有的节日里出现比较晚的一个，它原来是寒食节的一部分。寒食节一共有七天，清明节是寒食节的最后两天。寒食节的时候，大家都不能用火烧东西吃；清明节的活动就是扫墓。后来，寒食节慢慢地消失了，清明节的扫墓就变成了一年一次的传统，被越来越多的人知道和接受了。

清明节的时候，正好是春天，天气非常好。春天的太阳使人觉得很暖和、很舒服，到处都可以看到漂亮的花草和绿色的树木。扫墓是清明节最重要的事情。扫墓的地方一般都是在山上，每一家都会带许多东西去扫墓，路上到处都可以看到去扫墓的人。这是一个非常重要的日子。

什么是扫墓呢？就是每年到了这一天，大家都要到祖先的坟墓上去，纪念死去的亲人。大部分的墓都是在山上，一天又一天，坟墓前的草都长得很高。每年清明节的时候，大家就到祖先的坟墓前，把草拔一拔，把地扫一扫，把坟地整理整理，所以这一天的活动就叫做"扫墓"。

清明节是中国人纪念死去的亲人的日子，而扫墓就是一种纪念亲人的表现。到了山上，人们会先把长出来的草收拾干净，然后把带来的水果和许多吃的东西放在墓前。大家一起跪下安静地纪念死去的亲人，希望死去的亲人在地下过得幸福，也希望今天在世上的人生活得平安。

除了给死去的亲人带吃的东西以外，还要带很多的纸钱。纸钱不是真正的钱，而是假钱，是用来纪念死去的亲人的。扫墓的人在墓前烧这些纸钱，给死去的人用。中国人认为，人死去以后，在地下还会继续生活，所以也需要用钱，烧纸钱给亲人，就是希望他们在地下也有钱可以用。纸钱烧完了，活着的人也就把想念的心意带给了他们死去的亲人。

有时候，住在外地的亲人也会回来扫墓。平常大家都忙自己的工作，很难有机会见面，清明节的时候，亲人都回来了，正好可以在一起见见面。扫完墓以后，大家坐在一起休息，说说每个人家里的事情。亲人里面，有的人一年年地长大；有的人去年才刚刚结婚，今年就有孩子了……一年又一年，时间过得很快。看到自己的亲人越来越多，生活也越来越好，大家在一起就觉得很高兴，他们想，死去的亲人今天也会很高兴。

如果清明节的时候天气很好，大家在扫完墓以后，就会去一些地方随便玩玩。比方说，上山去看看风景，或者随便走走，或者和亲人在一起做一些简单的活动。这些活动不是因为大家想玩，而是因为它们可以帮助我们想想人生，认识生活的美丽。

清明节的这一天，有很多人会出来放风筝。风筝是什么东西呢？它是一个用纸做的可以飞的东西，一头用一条很长的线拉着，有风的时候，就会飞起来，人们拉住线，这样风筝就不会飞走了。风筝飞得越高，人们就会越高兴。

这时候，天上到处可以看到许多漂亮的风筝。很多风筝被做成各种不同的动物的样子，飞在天空中，天空就好像是一个动物园。这时，很多人坐在草地上，一边看着美丽的风景，一边吃着好吃的点心，在草地上玩得非常高兴。

很久很久以前，有一个人画了一张画。这是一张很长很长的中国画，这张画画得非常好，画里面都是中国人在清明节那天的活动。一共画了一千六百多个人和两百多个动物，画里的每一个人都不一样，有的人在看风景，有的人在买东西。画里面还有很多车和船。从这一张画里，我们可以知道过去人们的生活是什么样子的。

在中国的东南部，也许是地理的原因，也许是气候的原因，清明节那天的天气常常不好，经常会下雨。因为古时候一下雨，人们就不能出去工作，这样就有很多时间和家人在一起。雨天就好像代表了每个人的心情，下雨的时候，在外的人就会想念自己的家人，也会思考很多人生的事情。

清明节是一个纪念亲人的节日，也是一个大家感恩的日子。想念去世的那些人，感谢他们以前所做的事情，因为没有以前亲人们的努力，也就没有现在美好的生活。

清明节就是中国人纪念祖先的日子。

问题

1. 中国人把一年分成几个节气？
2. 清明节大概在每年的什么时候？
3. 清明节的时候有哪些活动？
4. 扫墓的时候要做哪些事情？
5. 扫完墓以后，大家会去做什么呢？
6. 那张有名的画，画了哪些东西？

生词

*	秋	qiū		autumn
*	季	jì		season; quarter(ly)
1.	节气	jiéqì	(N)	the 24 seasonal periods into which the lunar year is divided (each = 15 days)
2.	计算	jìsuàn	(V)	to calculate
*	计	jì		to calculate; a scheme, plot; a plan or program
*	概	gài		general, overall, roughly
3.	前后	qiánhòu	(TW)	or thereabouts (re. time)
4.	出现	chūxiàn	(V)	to appear, to emerge
5.	寒食节	Hánshíjié	(N)	Cold Food Festival (105th-107th day after the winter solstice during which food is supposed to be eaten cold)
*	寒	hán		cold, chilly, wintry
6.	扫墓	sǎo-mù	(VO)	(lit.:) to "sweep the grave" (i.e. to pay respects to ancestors)
*	墓	mù		a grave, a tomb
7.	消失	xiāoshī	(V)	to disappear, die out, vanish
	消	xiāo		to disappear, die out, vanish; to disperse, eliminate, remove
	失	shī		to lose; to neglect, let slip; an omission, mistake
8.	传统	chuántǒng	(N/SV)	tradition / traditional

Chapter 5: Tomb Sweeping Day

*	统	tǒng		to unify, unite; totally; to govern
*	越	yuè		the more; to cross over
9.	接受	jiēshòu	(V)	to accept
*	使	shǐ		to make, act; to use, employ
*	草	cǎo		grass, herb; draft (copy)
10.	树木	shùmù	(N)	trees
*	木	mù		wood; stupid, dumb-witted
11.	祖先	zǔxiān	(N)	(one's) ancestors, forefathers
*	祖	zǔ		ancestor; founder, originator
12.	坟墓	fénmù	(N)	a grave (or 墓 mù)
*	坟	fén		grave or mound
13*	拔	bá	(V)	to uproot, to pull out (e.g. teeth)
14.	坟地	féndì	(N)	graveyard, cemetery
15.	表现	biǎoxiàn	(N)	a show of (what one means or feels about something);
			(V)	to behave or perform (in an acceptable/unacceptable way)
16*	跪	guì	(V)	to kneel
*	安	ān		peaceful, quiet; to put/place
*	静	jìng		quiet & peaceful; motionless
17.	世上	shìshang	(PW)	on the earth, in the world
18.	纸钱	zhǐqián	(N)	paper money (burnt to the dead)
19.	想念	xiǎngniàn	(V)	to think affectionately of, to miss

20.	心意	xīnyì	(N)	(heartfelt) idea or intention
*	景	jǐng		scenery, view; circumstances
21.	人生	rénshēng	(N)	(meaning of) life
22.	风筝	fēngzheng	(N)	kite　　(放 = to fly [kites])
*	筝	zhēng		kite; kind of stringed instrument
*	线	xiàn		thread, wire; a line
*	拉	lā		to pull, drag; lengthen, elongate
23.	天空	tiānkōng	(PW)	the skies
24.	草地	cǎodì	(N)	grass meadow, pasture
*	船	chuán		boat, ship
25.	东南部	dōngnánbù	(PW)	south-east region/area
*	雨	yǔ		rain
26.	代表	dàibiǎo	(V/N)	to represent / representative
*	代	dài		be a substitute; generation, era
27.	思考	sīkǎo	(V)	to think deeply about, ponder
28.	感恩	gǎn'ēn	(VO)	to be thankful for
	感恩节	gǎn'ēnjié	(N)	Thanksgiving Day
*	恩	ēn		grace, favor, gratitude
*	努	nǔ		to exert (effort)
*	力	lì		strength, power; vigorously

Pattern: 不(是)……而是…… 　　not ..., but rather/instead ...

第六章　包饺子——热热闹闹地请客

许多人都说，中国的文化是"吃"的文化。为什么这样说呢？因为中国人不但很聪明，而且也很会吃。天上飞的东西，地上爬的东西，还有许许多多生活在水里的东西，每一样他们都能做成很好吃的中国菜。所以人们常说"吃在中国"。可见，中国菜在世界上是很有名的了。

但是，做中国菜很麻烦，常常要花很多时间。如果有客人来，主人就要花很长时间来做菜，这样就会很累，也会觉得做很多菜来请客不是最方便的办法。所以，另一种请客的方法就出现了。

这种方法又简单又方便，不用花很多时间，也不用花很多钱，更重要的是，做出来的东西很好吃。那么，这是什么方法呢？就是包饺子。饺子是中国北方人发明的。因为中国北方的天气比较冷，没有大米吃，他们吃的东西主要是面食，所以北方人会用面粉做各种各样的东西，饺子就是其中的一种。

做饺子要准备两样东西，饺子皮和饺子馅。饺子皮是用面粉做的，饺子馅是用菜和肉做的，用饺子皮把饺子馅包起来，这就是饺子。白白的饺子皮包着馅，样子又可爱又好看。以前要吃一顿饺子也不容易，因为饺子皮需要自己做，如果一个人吃二十个饺子，十个人吃饭就需要做两百多张饺子皮，而且，用菜和肉做馅也需要花很多时间。可是，做饺子还是比做菜简单多了。特别是现在的生活很方便，到处都可以买到饺子皮，做饺子请客就更容易了。

因为饺子很容易做，所以大家常常喜欢包饺子请客。有时候，主人还请客人一起来包饺子。包饺子以前，大家先把手洗干净，然后坐在一起一边包饺子，一边说说笑笑。主人和客人们在一起，可以聊很多很多话。用这种方法请客，大家都很高兴，也很热闹。有的时候，小孩子们也吵着要一起包，其实他们是想玩饺子，不是要包饺子。他们把饺子做成一个个奇怪的样子，白白的饺子在他们的手里变成了黑黑的饺子，这样的饺子怎么能吃呢？

所有的饺子都包好了以后，就可以开始下饺子了。饺子要怎么下呢？这个就更简单了。先把水烧开，然后把饺子放到水里，大概十分钟以后，等到一个个饺子都跑到水面上来以后，就可以捞出来吃了。看到热热的饺子，每个人的口水都快要流出来了。

每一个饺子都很漂亮，白白的、亮亮的，有时候，你还可以看见饺子里面的馅。你还会经常听见大家开玩笑说："这个漂亮的饺子一定是我包的！"要是看到一个奇怪的饺子，你也会听见别人开玩笑说："这个是你包的！"其实，不管饺子包成什么样子，吃起来都是一样地好吃。

包饺子虽然是一件简单的事，但是中国人却可以用不同的方法来做，比方说，用不同的肉，或者用不同的菜。饺子馅不一样，吃起来味道也会不一样。就这样，各种不同口味的饺子就出现了。

不但饺子里包的东西不一样，饺子的吃法也不同。用水下饺子是最常见的吃法。因为是用开水煮的，所以叫做"水饺"。饺子也可以不用水煮，用油来煎，那又是另一种饺子了，味道很特别，也很好吃。有的人喜欢吃水饺，也有的人特别喜欢吃用油煎的饺子。

从前饺子是过年的时候才吃的。包饺子的时候，有的人会故意把硬币包在饺子里，如果谁吃到了包着硬币的饺子，人们就相信他今年的生活会过得很好。所以，过年时如果你有机会到中国人家里吃饺子，最好先问问今天包的饺子里有没有包硬币。千万不要吃得太快，要不然你的肚子可能就会出问题了。

现在，人们不管什么时候都可以吃饺子。市场上可以买到已经做好的饺子皮和饺子馅。也有人做生意，卖已经包好的饺子，还有一些工厂做饺子，一下子就可以做出很多饺子。所以，吃饺子越来越方便了，家里有客人来了，不用几分钟就可以有又热又好吃的饺子吃了。

饺子做起来虽然很简单，吃起来却很好吃，而且它也代表着主人的心意，这就是饺子最特别的地方了。大家一起吃饺子，一起聊天，一起开玩笑，因为中国人最喜欢热闹了。如果有一天，中国人请你到他家吃饺子，你只要做一件事情——就是答应他吧！

问题

1. 中国菜很有名，为什么又出现另一种请客的方法呢？
2. 包饺子请客有什么好处？
3. 包饺子的时候要准备哪两样东西？
4. 饺子的做法是什么？
5. 中国人想出什么不同的方法来做饺子？
6. 中国人为什么要把硬币包在饺子里？
7. 现在吃饺子，为什么越来越方便了？
8. 饺子特别的地方在哪里？

生 词

*	饺	jiǎo		stuffed dumpling
*	聪	cōng		clever, astute, bright
*	界	jiè		to demarcate; domain, territory
*	麻	má		numb; hemp; pock-marked
*	烦	fán		annoy, trouble, worry, be vexed
1.	主人	zhǔrén	(N)	host(ess) [polite]; master, lord
2.	发明	fāmíng	(V/N)	to invent / an invention
3.	大米	dàmǐ	(N)	white rice or pearl rice
4.	面粉	miànfěn	(N)	flour
5.	其中	qízhōng	(N)	of which, of those/them [also: among, in the midst (of)]
*	皮	pí		skin, fur, leather, rind; naughty
6.*	馅	xiàn	(N)	stuffing, filling (for dumplings)
*	吵	chǎo		to quarrel, to dispute, to row; to disturb, to annoy
7.	下饺子	xià jiǎozi	(VO)	to place the *jiaozi* in the water
8.	烧开	shāokāi	(RV)	(of water) to bring to the boil
9.	水面上	shuǐmiànshang	(PW)	on the surface of the water
10.*	捞	lāo	(V)	to pull or drag out of the water
11.	口水	kǒushuǐ	(N)	saliva
	流口水	liú kǒushuǐ	(VO)	to make one's mouth water

46 Chapter 6: Stuffing Dumplings

*	流	liú		to flow, wander; a division, rank
12.	要是	yàoshi	(A)	if
13.*	却	què	(A)	however, but, still, yet
*	煮	zhǔ		to boil, to stew; to cook (meals)
14.	煮饭	zhǔ fàn	(VO)	to cook a meal
15.	油	yóu	(N)	oil
*	煎	jiān		to fry (in fat or oil)
16.	硬币	yìngbì	(N)	coins (i.e. hard money as opposed to paper money)
*	硬	yìng		hard, stiff; inflexible, rigid
*	币	bì		currency, money
*	厂	chǎng		factory, workshop
17.	一下子	yíxiàzi	(N)	(in) a moment, in a short space of time

第七章　三代同堂

很久以前，中国能有机会读书的人不是很多，所以，孩子们从小就跟着父母学做事。如果爸爸是种田的，孩子们也就跟着学种田；如果爸爸是做生意的，孩子们也就跟着学做生意。等到孩子长大了，结了婚、生了自己的小孩，他们还是会和爸爸妈妈住在一起，不会离开原来的家。这种祖父母、父母和孩子们住在一起的家庭，就是"三代同堂"。

三代同堂的家庭在中国是很常见的。以前中国人认为人越多越好，所以每个家庭都生很多孩子。孩子们长大结婚以后，大家还是住在一起，孩子的孩子又继续生很多孩子，就这样，一个家庭越来越大，家里的人也就越来越多。有的时候，一个家庭已经不是三代同堂，而是四代同堂，或者是五代同堂了。大家认为家庭越大，就越有福气，也不怕别人来找麻烦了。

以前的皇帝也很喜欢大家庭，认为大家庭有很多好处。古时候，有一个家庭有七百多人，所以皇帝就去看他们，还送给他们很多礼物。那时候，国家希望每个家庭都生很多孩子，因为人越多，国家就会越强，也就不怕别的国家来找麻烦了。

第七章　三代同堂

三代同堂中的第一代是祖父母。他们在家里的地位是最高的，家庭中重大的决定都要经过他们的同意才可以。他们的年纪最大，知道的事情也比较多，所以当大家有问题的时候，都会去问他们，祖父母也会很高兴地帮忙，把所知道的事情都告诉孩子们。

三代同堂的第二代是父母亲，他们做的工作最多：一方面要照顾年老的祖父母，关心他们的身体，让他们生活得快乐；另一方面，又要照顾孩子，注意他们的功课。做父母的，白天要努力工作，晚上也要做很多家里的事情。他们的身体常常是家中最好的，但是他们做的工作也是最辛苦的。

三代同堂中的第三代是小孩子。他们是最幸福的，平时父母亲会照顾他们，如果父母亲出去工作了，祖父母就会照顾他们。祖父母是最喜欢小孩子的，他们要什么祖父母就会给他们什么。如果小孩子做错了什么事，让父母亲很生气，祖父母就会出来为孩子们说好话。小孩子真是家里最快乐的人了！

三代同堂有什么好处呢？以前中国人很多都是种田的，种田最需要的就是家里人的帮助，所以家里有这么多的人，就可以一起帮忙做。祖父母可以帮着做些简单的事，辛苦的事就让父母亲来做，小孩子当然也要帮助大人干一些简单的家务。这样，一家人一起做，事情很快就做完了。

到了晚上，吃完了晚饭，事情都做完了，一家人就都坐到院子里。大家在院子里一块儿说说话、休息休息，这时候，祖父母就会把他们以前听过的故事，讲给小孩子听，这些故事也都是祖父母的祖父母告诉他们的。孩子们越听越喜欢听，天天都要祖父母讲故事给他们听！

祖父母照顾孩子们，父母亲照顾祖父母，小孩子们让祖父母很快乐，因为每个人都需要别人的关心和照顾。中国人常常告诉自己的孩子，一定要孝顺父母。那么，什么是孝顺父母呢？就是要听父母的话，不能让父母难过。在三代同堂的家庭里，小孩子从小就看着父母是怎样孝顺祖父母的，慢慢地，等到他们长大了，也会很孝顺父母。就这样，一代接一代，大家都学会了孝顺。

中国人是很看重家庭的。如果家里有一个人做了好事，大家就都很高兴，好像全家人都做了好事一样；如果家里有一个人做了错事或坏事，大家就会觉得全家人都做了错事或坏事。所以，家里的每一个人都常常很小心，不希望做出对不起大家的事情。

现在中国的家庭不像以前那样生很多的孩子了。以前的人有一种想法，生孩子是为了年老以后，可以有人照顾。现在这样的想法慢慢变了，可是，三代同堂的家庭还是很多，这是为什么呢？其实中国人孝顺父母、照顾小孩并不一定是希望得到什么好处,最重要的是一家人在一起的那种快乐。"家"在中国人的心目中永远是最重要的。

问题

1. 什么叫做"三代同堂"?
2. 古时候的国家为什么会希望大家多生小孩呢?
3. 三代中,谁的地位最高,为什么?
4. 三代中,谁做的工作最多,为什么?
5. 三代中,谁最幸福,为什么?
6. 三代同堂有什么好处?
7. 事情忙完了,晚上大家都做些什么事?
8. 为什么一个人做错了事会觉得对不起家人?

生 词

1. 三代同堂 sāndàitóngtáng (PH) — three generations under the same roof

   代 dài (M) — generation

   * 堂 táng — hall, meeting/reception room; relatives of the same grandfather

2. 做事 zuò-shì (VO) — do work of a more casual nature (工作 is work of a more formal kind)

   * 田 tián — (rice) fields, cultivated land

3. 等到 děng dào (V) — by the time when, until

4. 祖父母 zǔfùmǔ (N) — grandparents

   祖父 zǔfù (N) — grandfather

   祖母 zǔmǔ (N) — grandmother

5. 见(到) jiàn(dào) (V) — to see

6. 福气 fúqì (N) — blessing, good luck

   * 怕 pà — fear (that), be afraid of; perhaps

7. 找麻烦 zhǎo máfan (VO) — to pick on somebody, find fault [or to ask for trouble]

   * 强 qiáng — strong, powerful, vigorous

8. 重大 zhòngdà (SV) — major, significant, important [or serious, grave]

9. 当……的时候 dāng ... de shíhou — when

   * 顾 gù — to care for, look after; look at

10.	年老	niánlǎo	(SV)	aged
*	功	gōng		effort; function; merit
11.	干(活儿)	gàn (huór)	(VO)	to work, to do a job
*	干	gàn		to do, to attend to some matter
12.	家务	jiāwù	(N)	domestic chores, housework
*	讲	jiǎng		to talk, speak; to explain; to be fussy about
13.	孝顺	xiàoshùn	(V/SV)	to be filial to one's parents
*	孝	xiào		be filial to one's parents
*	顺	shùn		submit to, obey; smooth-going
14.	听	tīng	(V)	to obey, be obedient to
15.	接	jiē	(V)	follow on after, one after another
	接着	jiēzhe	(A)	thereupon, shortly afterwards
16.	看重	kànzhòng	(V)	to regard as important
*	坏	huài		bad; broken down; vicious
17.	对不起	duìbuqǐ	(V)	to let (someone) down badly
18.	心目(中)	xīnmù(zhōng)	(PW)	(in) one's heart or mind

第八章　泼水节——西南民俗

中国是一个很大的国家，从古到今，生活着很多不同的民族。在中国，人口最多的民族叫做汉族，汉族人也叫汉人。前面的课文里，大家读到的一些风俗大多数是汉族的风俗。除了汉族以外，别的民族人口比较少，所以叫做少数民族。那么，这些少数民族是不是也有许多特别的风俗呢？让我们一起来看看吧！

在中国的西南部，那里有很多高山和大河。因为山很高，水很深，从一个地方到另一个地方去很不方便，所以一个地方的人很少和住在别的地方的人来往，日子久了，每个地方都慢慢地有了自己的文化和生活习惯。后来，这些地方的人民就变成了一个个小的民族。中国的西南部是少数民族最多的地方。

在中国的西南，有一个少数民族，他们有一个特别的节日，叫做"泼水节"。每到泼水节的这一天，大家都要把水泼到别人的身上去，被泼到水的人不但不生气，反而还会很高兴。怎么会有这么奇怪的节日呢？传说这个节日是从一个古老的故事开始的……

很久很久以前，在这个地方住着一个很可怕的人，他经常会出来吃人，住在这里的人都很怕他。这个人有七个美丽的妻子，她们也很害怕她们的丈夫，很不喜欢他。为了帮助这里的人民可以平平安安地过日子，有一天晚上，她们就把这个可怕的丈夫杀死了。

这个可怕的人虽然死了，可是奇怪的是，他的头却还活着。七个妻子就把他的头扔到了河里。可是头一被扔到河里，河水就变得很热，把河里的鱼都热死了。她们又把头扔在地上，地上就不长东西了。最后她们七个人只好换着拿他的头，一天换一个人，被换下来的那个人，大家就赶快给她泼水，洗去她身上的脏东西。后来，人们为了感谢她们七个人，就有了一年一次的泼水节。

这个地方的泼水节就像是汉族的新年。这时候，到处都有各种好玩的活动。泼水节的第一天不泼水，而是在大河里比赛划船。谁得到第一名，大家就都为他高兴，有的人唱歌，有的人跳舞。到了第二天，就开始泼水了！不管男人、女人，还是小孩、老人，大家都一起向别人泼水。你泼我，我泼你，谁被泼得越多就表示他越有福气，因为水可以帮助除掉一切不好的东西，第二年的生活就会过得更好。所以，如果你到了那里，身上被别人泼了水，千万不要生气，反而应该高兴，最好你也给别人多泼一些水。

泼水节的晚上更热闹了。所有的人都会到同一个地方去，歌声、笑声到处都是，有的人跳舞，有的人拍手。有些人太高兴了，喝了酒，就一边唱歌一边跳舞，好像忘记了自己是谁；还有很多很多的人来到这里，就是要看看泼水节。就这样，这个地方一直到很晚很晚才会安静下来。

在泼水节的时候，还有一个很特别的活动。如果一个人爱上了另一个人，就会把一件自己喜欢的东西送给对方。要是有人送给你一件东西，这个人一定是喜欢上你了。在这个活动中，有的人还会趁别人不注意的时候，拿走他的东西。这也是因为他爱上了对方。如果你有机会参加泼水节，发现自己的东西不见了，说不定就是有人喜欢上你了！

中国西南还有很多其他的少数民族，他们也有很多特别的节日。有一个少数民族，他们住在又高又冷的山上，在那里，洗澡很不方便，所以他们很少洗澡。但是他们有"洗澡节"，洗澡节的时候，天气很暖和，河水也不那么冷了，大家就一起去河里洗澡。因为人很多，原来很干净的河水一下子都变成黑色的了。一年里能够洗澡的机会不多，所以一到洗澡节，大家就都高兴得不得了！

还有一些少数民族的节日有唱歌比赛或者骑马比赛。西南的少数民族都爱唱歌、骑马，更喜欢和大家快乐地在一起。他们也有自己民族的新年，和汉族新年的时间不一样。新年的时候，大家会喝一点酒，也会吃一些自己民族特有的东西。

中国土地很大，人口很多，民族也很多。从过去到现在，不同的民族都有自己不同的文化。它们的节日不一样，活动也不一样，可是，有一点是一样的，就是大家都希望过得平安、快乐。后来有些不同民族的人慢慢地也分不太清了，他们都变成了一家人。

问题

1. 中国最大的民族是哪一个民族？
2. 如果你有地图，你能找出中国的西南吗？
3. 那里是不是有很多的高山和大河？
4. 泼水节的第一天做些什么事？
5. 泼水节的第二天做些什么事？
6. 在泼水节时被泼了水，为什么不会生气呢？
7. 泼水节的晚会，大家做些什么事？
8. 泼水节的时候，为什么会有人拿别人的东西呢？
9. 什么是"洗澡节"呢？

生 词

1.	泼水节	Pōshuǐjié	(N)	Water Splashing Festival
*	泼	pō		to pour, to sprinkle
2.	民俗	mínsú	(N)	customs & practices of a people
3.	民族	mínzú	(N)	an ethnic group; a nation
	少数民族	shǎoshùmínzú	(N)	minority people group
	少数	shǎoshù	(N)	a minority
*	数	shù / shǔ		number; several / to count
*	族	zú		tribe, clan; family/class (of); a race (of people);
4.	汉族	Hànzú	(N)	the Han Chinese (as a people group)
	汉人	Hànrén	(N)	the Han Chinese
5.	大多数	dàduōshù	(N)	the majority (of)
*	河	hé		river, waterway
*	深	shēn		deep (water); dark (color); profound (idea)
6.	来往	láiwǎng	(N)	social intercourse
7.	人民	rénmín	(N)	the people (as opposed to the rulers or the government)
8.	反而	fǎn'ér	(A)	on the contrary
9.	古老	gǔlǎo	(SV)	ancient, antiquated
10.	害怕	hàipà	(SV)	fearful, to be scared/afraid of

*	害	hài		to harm, to injure, to damage
11.	杀死	shāsǐ	(RV)	to kill, to murder
*	杀	shā		to kill, put to death, slaughter
*	扔	rēng		to throw, to hurl; to abandon, to discard
*	换	huàn		to change; to exchange
*	赶	gǎn		to hurry, to hasten; to pursue, catch up with; to expel
*	脏	zāng		dirty, filthy
*	赛	sài		to compete, contest, tournament
*	划	huá		to row (a boat); an oar
12.	表示	biǎoshì	(V)	to show, to indicate, to express
*	示	shì		to show, indicate, demonstrate
13.	除掉	chúdiào	(V)	to remove, to get rid of (prejudices, obstacles, etc.)
*	切	qiè / qiē		be close to / to slice, carve, cut
14.	歌声	gēshēng	(N)	the sound of singing
*	声	shēng		voice, sound; fame, make known
15.	拍手	pāi-shǒu	(VO)	to clap (with the hands)
*	拍	pāi		to strike with the hand, to pat, to slap; music beat
16.	爱上	àishàng	(RV)	to love (see CME lesson 52 1.3)
	喜欢上	xǐhuānshang	(RV)	to like, have taken a fancy for

*	参	cān		to participate in; to visit
17.	说不定	shuōbudìng	(EX)	maybe, who can say, perhaps, can't say for certain
*	澡	zǎo		to wash, to bathe
18.	特有的	tèyǒude	(SV)	unique (to ...), special, exclusive to
*	土	tǔ		earth, soil; native, local; land, ground, territory
19.	点	diǎn	(M)	a point (e.g. in a lecture)
20.	晚会	wǎn huì	(N)	evening gathering, meeting or party

第九章　古时候的教育

两千五百多年前，在中国，有一个很有名的人叫孔子，他提出了一些很重要的思想。他认为，不管一个人有没有钱或者有没有地位，都应该去读书，学习做人和做事的道理。在教育的方法上，对不同特点的孩子，应该用不同的方法教育。孔子的想法非常好，大家都认为他是中国古代第一位伟大的老师。他的想法是中国教育思想的开始，一直到现在，这些思想还是很有道理、很有用的。

中国人教育孩子，最重要的，是希望小孩子知道怎么做人。一个有礼貌的人就应该知道什么时候该站着，什么时候该坐着，做每一件事情，都要有礼貌。他们都相信，一个受过教育的人才可能把自己和家里的事情做好；一个能把自己和家里的事做好的人才可能把国家的事做好；一个能把国家的事做好的人才可能让世界更和平。所以要教育一个人，就要从小事情开始教起，以后他才能做大事情。

古时候，有的人在学校学习，有的人在家里学习。古代的学校和现在的学校也不一样，公共的学校很少，很多学校都是老师自己办的。学校比较小，学生也不多，来读书的人年纪也都不一样，有的人从小就在学校读书，有的人长大以后才来读书。

来读书的人都是男孩子，那时候很少有女孩子可以读书。中国古时候有一个很美的爱情故事。故事是说一个女孩非常想到学校去读书，可是那时候去读书的人都是男孩。她就穿上男孩的衣服，让自己看起来像男孩一样。结果，在学校里，她认识了另外一个男同学，刚开始这个男同学并不知道她是一个女孩子，他们俩一起读书、一起玩。后来，他们俩的故事变成了一个爱情故事。

古代的教育需要人们读历史上的人写的书，书里有诗，还有很多做人做事的道理。在学校，除了读书以外，老师还会用其他的方法来教育孩子，像弹琴、下棋、写字和画画等等，因为大家都相信这些教育可以帮助一个人变成真正有用的人。

对中国人来说，弹琴是一个很好的教育方法。学琴的时候，要很用心才可以弹出美好的音乐。听到美好的琴声，人们常常就会有很好的心情。另外，一个人可以用琴声把他的心情表现出来，使自己和别人都可以从琴声中得到一些做人的道理。

下棋是另一种教育方法。中国人经常喜欢下围棋，那么，下围棋能给孩子们什么帮助呢？它能帮助小孩子在遇到困难的时候，不紧张，也不着急，能够安静地去思考；下围棋也可以帮助孩子们在事情发生变化的时候，把问题看得更清楚；还可以帮助他们得到处理问题的信心和能力。

写字也是教育孩子的一种方法。中国人常说：字如其人。这句话的意思是说，看一个人写的字，差不多就知道他这个人怎么样。可是，古时候的人写字不像现在这么方便。那时候，大家都是用毛笔写字，写字时如果用力太大，字就会又黑又难看；写字时用力太小，字就会又细又不好看。所以用毛笔写字时，手的力气要刚刚好才可以，写字时也一定要用心，而且要常写。所以，历史上很多有名的人每天都要练习很长时间。

画画也是学习的好机会。可是，你有没有发现中国古时候的画很特别？那种画叫中国画，或者叫国画。国画中画的东西和真的东西不太一样。因为中国画主要不是去画那些我们看得见的山、水和花草树木的本来的样子，而是去画人们心里想的那些东西，所以画画是一种教育的好方法。它可以让孩子们有很多的机会去想象，使他们认识到生活的美好并且热爱生活，同时对学习产生更大的兴趣。所以，那些喜欢画画的孩子们的心会变得更细、更美丽。

不管是弹琴、下棋、写字还是画画，都能帮助一个孩子健康成长，使他得到真正的教育。它们可以教会孩子们不会因为一点点的小事而难过，也不会为一点点的困难而失去信心；

遇到问题的时候，能够安静下来想办法；事情很多的时候，也能够把它们一件一件地完成。

生活里的每一件小事都可以用来教育孩子。但是古时候能读书的人并不多。有的人从小就要帮助父母做事，没有时间和钱来读书，也不认识字。虽然这样，中国的父母还是会告诉自己的孩子做人的道理。家就是孩子们的学校，父母就是他们的老师，生活中的每一件事情都是他们要学习的功课。所以，有的人在学校读书，有的人在家里学习，但是每个人都希望自己的孩子成为一个有用的人。

问题

1. 为什么教育一个人要从小事教起？
2. 古时候的学校是怎么样的？
3. 古时候，在学校都学些什么？
4. 弹琴有什么好处？
5. 下棋为什么可以教育一个人呢？
6. 写毛笔字时，要注意什么？
7. 画画为什么也是学习的好方法？
8. 没到学校读书的人，是怎么学习的呢？

生 词

*	育	yù		to educate; to raise (children); to give birth to, to breed;
*	孔	kǒng		(family name) / a hole/opening
1.	思想	sīxiǎng	(N/V)	ideological inclination, ideology; thoughts, ideas / to think about
2.	做人	zuò-rén	(VO)	to conduct oneself appropriately
3.	道理	dàolǐ	(N)	teaching; right or proper way
	有道理	yǒu dàolǐ	(SV)	reasonable, plausible
4.	特点	tèdiǎn	(N)	special features or characteristics
5.	古代	gǔdài	(TW)	ancient times
6.	伟大	wěidà	(SV)	great, extraordinary (as in: Beethoven was a great musician)
*	伟	wěi		extraordinary, great; gigantic
7.	有用	yǒu yòng	(SV)	useful; beneficial
8.	有礼貌	yǒu lǐmào	(SV)	to be courteous, well mannered
	礼貌	lǐmào	(N)	good manners, politeness
*	貌	mào		facial appearance; manner
9.	受教育	shòu jiàoyù	(VO)	to receive an education
10.	和平	hépíng	(N) (SV)	(world) peace (e.g. Peace Mission) peaceful (living)
11.	公共	gōnggòng	(BF)	public (relations, health, etc.)
12.	爱情	àiqíng	(BF)	love (between man & woman)

Chapter 9: Education in Ancient Times

13.*	俩	liǎ	(NU)	the two; a couple
14.	弹琴	tán-qín	(VO)	to play a stringed instrument (e.g. piano; but *not* with a bow)
*	弹	tán / dàn		to play (a stringed instrument sounded by *snapping* action); to rebound / a pellet
*	琴	qín		a stringed musical instrument
*	棋	qí		chess
15.	用心	yòngxīn	(SV)	(do sthg.) attentively or intently
16.	围棋	wéiqí	(N)	"Encirclement Chess" or "Go"
*	围	wéi		to encircle, surround, hem in
*	遇	yù		to encounter, meet up with; to treat; opportunity, luck
*	困	kùn		difficult, hard; poor; tired, weary, fatigued
*	紧	jǐn		tight, firm; urgent, pressing
*	急	jí		urgent, hurried; anxious, worried; quick(ly)
17.	处理	chǔlǐ	(V)	to deal with, sort out (problems)
18.	能力	nénglì	(N)	ability, capability
19.	毛笔	máobǐ	(N)	Chinese writing brush
*	毛	máo		(body) hair; woolen; dime
20.	用力	yòng-lì	(VO)	exert oneself, put forth strength
21.	力气	lìqi	(N)	physical strength

22.	想象	xiǎngxiàng	(V)	to imagine, to suppose that
	想象力	xiǎngxiànglì	(N)	(power of) imagination
23.	热爱	rè'ài	(V)	to love passionately/fervently
			(N)	passionate love, deep attachment
24.	产生	chǎnshēng	(V)	to produce, to give rise to
*	产	chǎn		to produce, to bring about; to bear (offspring)
*	健	jiàn		healthy, strong; vigorous; capable
*	康	kāng		healthy
25.	成长	chéngzhǎng	(V/N)	to grow (in maturity) / growth
26.	教会	jiāohuì	(RV)	to teach (someone) to master (something)
27.	失去	shīqù	(V)	to lose ...
28.	想办法	xiǎng bànfǎ	(VO)	to think of a way/solution
29.	完成	wánchéng	(V)	to complete, to accomplish
30.	认识字	rènshi zì	(VO)	to be literate, be able to read

第十章　端午节——龙舟和粽子

大概在两千三百多年前，中国分成了七个小国家，这七个小国家经常打来打去，谁也不让谁。在他们当中，有一个小国家在中国的南方，叫楚国。楚国有一个很爱国的人，他的名字叫<u>屈原</u>。屈原帮助国王和国家做了很多的事情，他常发现国家的问题，也告诉国王应该怎么做，怎样处理。他是一个很有才能的人，大家都很喜欢他。

国王一直也很喜欢屈原，因为他给了国王很多的帮助，可是，有些人不喜欢屈原。他们看到国王特别喜欢屈原，心里很不高兴，所以就在国王的面前说了很多屈原的坏话。国王听了以为是真的，很生气，慢慢地就变得不喜欢屈原了。

国王有一个不好的习惯，就是最喜欢听别人说好听的话，如果有人向国王说好听的话，国王就会很喜欢他。有一些坏人知道国王的这个习惯，就天天向他说好听的话。国王越听越高兴，就常和这些坏人在一起，所以屈原说的话，国王越来越不喜欢听了。有一天，国王因为屈原说的话很不高兴，一生气，就把屈原赶到了很远很远的地方，屈原的生活一下子就完全改变了。

屈原每天待在家里,心里非常难过。他难过的时候就写诗,写完诗就更难过了。他写了很多很多的诗,在这些诗里写出了他的心情、他对国家的爱和想对国王说的话。可是,国王一点也不知道屈原离开以后的事情。后来屈原的心情越来越不好,他觉得活在世上已经没有什么意思了。他来到一条河边,看着河水,想着国家的事情,就跳到河里去了。他希望这样国王能明白他的心,也希望用死来告诉国王,要好好地把国家的事情做好,不要再听坏人的话了。

认识屈原的人都知道他是一个很爱国的人,当他们听到屈原跳河了,就都跑到河边来找他。有的人坐着小木船在河里到处找,有的人在河边喊他的名字,可是,大家再也找不到他了。人们怕他的身体被鱼吃了,所以想出一个办法:用一种叶子把米包起来,放到河里去。这种叶子包米的东西就是后来中国人吃的粽子。人们希望鱼都来吃粽子,而不去吃他的身体。

因为屈原死的那天正好是中国农历的五月初五,所以以后每年的五月五日,人们都会想到屈原这位爱国诗人。大家都希望屈原并没有死,有一天还能找到他,所以到了这一天,很多人还会坐着船,把粽子放到河里去。日子久了,知道的人越来越多,每年的这个时候,在中国很多地方都有许许多多的人来纪念屈原,所以后来这一天就变成了中国一个很大的节日,叫端午节。

端午节是中国三大节日之一，它在每年中国农历的五月初五，因为是五月五日，所以很久以前人们就把这一天叫做端午节。后来人们知道屈原已经不在世上了，所以每年这个时候就不再把粽子扔到河里去了。但是端午节的时候，每一家还是会包很多的粽子吃，大家包粽子、吃粽子，一边想念屈原，一边告诉孩子们这位爱国诗人的故事。

端午节的时候，正好农民不太忙，可以休息。这时候，人们已经不再划船找屈原了，但是大家还是喜欢用划船这种活动来纪念这位爱国诗人。所以，每年五月初五，在中国的许多地方都有划船比赛。中国人最喜欢龙，因为他们认为自己是龙的后代。后来的人就把船做成了一种特别的样子，船头就像是一个龙的头，船的外面画了很多漂亮的颜色，他们把这种船叫做"龙舟"，每条龙舟上可以坐十几个人。每年端午节，大河上都有许多龙舟比赛，比赛一开始，大家都努力地向前划，因为大家都想得第一名。

今天，端午节已经是中国人的一个重要节日了。这一天中国人都会想到吃粽子，虽然现在到处都可以买到粽子，许多人家，特别是农村家庭还是喜欢自己包粽子吃。如果有人在外面工作，不能回家，爸爸妈妈就会请人带粽子给他吃。有的人是一个人，没有成家，或者家在很远的地方，他的朋友就会请他吃粽子，要不然，他就自己到外面去买粽子吃。所以，端午节的时候如果没吃粽子，大家就会觉得很奇怪，好像忘了做一件重要的事情。

古时候,如果有龙舟比赛,大家都会跑来看热闹,而且河边有人卖东西,也有人买东西。比赛开始的时候,河边更是热闹,人声、水声、笑声和叫声一起响起来,非常有意思!现在,龙舟比赛还是很多地方过端午节的一个重要活动。

端午节的时候,一般是最热的时候。这时候,农民可以在家里休息一段时间,准备接下来要忙的事情。因为天热,人容易累,没有力气种田,所以农民在这个时候经常要喝一些酒,听说喝了酒,人不容易生病,也不怕热。这应该不是想要喝酒的借口!

端午节是中国人一年中很大的一个节日,它使人想起爱国诗人屈原,屈原的故事又让人明白为什么中国人每年要划龙舟和吃粽子。

问题

1. 请简单地说出端午节的故事。
2. 端午节这一天,大家为什么要划龙舟、包粽子?
3. 你知道中国有哪三大节日吗?
4. 你知道龙舟比赛是什么样的吗?
5. 农民为什么会有时间参加龙舟比赛?
6. 端午节为什么要喝酒?
7. 屈原是谁?

生 词

*	舟	zhōu		boat, ship
*	粽	zòng		glutinous rice tamale
1.	打来打去	dǎ lái dǎ qù	(PH)	to fight back & forth
2.	让	ràng	(V)	to give way to, yield, back down
3.	当中	dāngzhōng	(PW)	in the middle (of)
4.	楚国	Chǔ guó	(PW)	the Country of Chu
5.	爱国	àiguó	(SV)	patriotic
*	屈	qū		(Chinese name); to humiliate; to bend, to flex
6.	国王	guówáng	(N)	king, monarch
7.	才能	cáinéng	(N)	talent, abilities
8.	面前	miànqián	(PW)	in (someone's) presence, before
9.	赶	gǎn	(V)	to drive (out/away), to expel
10.	改变	gǎibiàn	(V) (N)	to change, alter, transform; a change, transformation
*	改	gǎi		to change, alter, modify
11*	喊	hǎn	(V)	to shout, to cry out, to scream
12*	初	chū		first; original; junior; early [here used when counting the first 10 days of the lunar month]
13.	之一	zhī yī		one of ...
*	之	zhī		of (= possessive particle)

14.	后代	hòudài	(N)	descendants
*	村	cūn		village, hamlet
15.	成家	chéng jiā	(VO)	to become a family man (i.e. to get married)
*	响	xiǎng		to sound, to ring; a sound, echo
*	段	duàn		Measure for a period of time; section, division; paragraph
16.	借口	jièkǒu	(N)	an excuse

第十一章　古老的习俗——坐月子和小脚女人

很久以来，中国文化里就有很多特别的习惯。这些文化习惯有些是好的，有些是不好的；有些我们今天可以理解，有些我们不能理解；还有一些是现在的人不能接受的。但是不管怎么样，很多的文化习惯大家还是从小就跟着做，那么，中国人今天还有哪些特别的文化习惯呢？

比方说，关于生孩子这件事。古时候，孩子还没有出生以前，妈妈就要注意很多事情。如果肚子里有了孩子，就不能随便拿房子里的东西。因为那时候的人们认为，如果妈妈不小心，随便拿了房子里的东西，小孩子生出来以后就可能长得很奇怪，可能会多一只眼睛或者少一只手。一直到现在，如果有人生了奇怪的孩子，别人还会认为一定是妈妈不小心拿了什么东西了。

有一个古老的文化习惯，可能今天还影响着每一个中国家庭，这就是"坐月子"。什么是"坐月子"呢？"坐月子"就是生完孩子以后，妈妈要待在家里一个月才可以出门。这是因为，生孩子以前，妈妈辛苦了十个月，生完孩子以后，妈妈的身体又很不好,所以她要在家休息一个月。有人会问:"这不是一件很好的事情吗?"可是,要在家里整整待一个月,那并不是妈妈很喜欢的一件事情!

这一个月里,妈妈要吃很多东西来补身体。这些东西很多都是跟中药一起烧出来的,中药烧的鱼,中药烧的鸡和中药烧的猪肉。妈妈刚刚吃完一条鱼,家里人又在做另一条给她吃。刚刚吃完一只鸡,又一只烧好了放在她的面前。好吃的东西吃得太多,也会变得不好吃。年轻的妈妈们虽然不喜欢,但是还是一定要吃下去。因为听老人们说,坐月子对身体是有帮助的,月子坐得好,妈妈的身体才会好,下一次生孩子的时候,孩子也才会长得健康。

坐月子的时候,还有很多要注意的事情:妈妈不能吃冷东西、不能拿重东西、不能吹风、不能洗头。老祖母天天都会告诉她,不能做这个,不能做那个;一定要吃这个,一定要吃那个。想想看,一个月不洗头,是一件多可怕的事情,所以很多妈妈都觉得,在家里待一个月太长了!

古时候,特别的文化习惯还有很多,包小脚就是最奇怪的一种了。包小脚就是把女人的脚用布紧紧地包起来,不让脚长大。为什么要包小脚呢?传说有这样一个故事。很久很久以前,有一个皇帝很喜欢一个女人,这个女人个子小小的,很会跳舞。有一天,这个女人用布把脚包得小小的,跳起舞来特别好看，皇帝看了，高兴得不得了，就要求全国所有的女人都包小脚。皇帝说，脚越小，女人就越好看。

从这以后，女人包小脚就成了一个传统。为了让脚变得很小，女人在四五岁的时候，就得把脚包起来，几天才能打开一次，把脚洗一洗，洗干净了，还要再包起来。最难的是，每一次一定要把脚包得和原来一样小。可是，女孩子越长越大，脚也越长越大，脚包小了，她们的脚就很疼。很多时候她们疼得站也站不好，坐也坐不住，有的人就哭着跟爸爸妈妈说，不要再包小脚了。但是爸爸妈妈也会哭着对她说："孩子！现在你如果不包小脚，以后就没有人会喜欢你，也没有人敢娶你了。"

就这样，一年过了一年，女人的脚都包得紧紧的，长大以后她们的脚真的就很小，只有七八公分长。因为她们的脚非常小，所以站不了很久，也走不了多远。平常走路的时候，还需要人来帮忙，走起路来，就像一朵花被风吹来吹去。那时候，人们认为小脚的女人最好看，所以从前的中国女人都有包小脚的习惯。

现在，人们知道的事情越来越多。大家都知道包脚不但对身体不好，而且也不是一个可以让人接受的文化习惯。女人不一定必须包脚，小脚女人也不一定好看，所以慢慢地，女孩子就不再包小脚了。今天在有些地方，人们还能看见有些包过小脚的老太太,但是从年轻的女人们的脚上已经看不到这个古老的文化习惯了。

很多人发现,中国社会有很多的文化习惯都是和女人有关的。因为中国文化比较重视男人,所以男人可以做很多他想做的事情,可是女人就有很多事情不能做。现在时代不一样了,中国社会变化很大,虽然男女还是不太平等,但是现代的中国女人已经比以前幸福多了。

问题

1. 为什么肚子里有孩子的妈妈不能随便拿房间里的东西?
2. 什么叫"坐月子"?
3. "坐月子"的时候,妈妈都吃些什么东西?
4. "坐月子"的时候要注意什么?
5. 古时候,中国的女人为什么要包小脚?
6. 小脚女人怎么走路?
7. 为什么现在还有一些老祖母有小脚呢?

生 词

1. 习俗　　　xísú　　　　　(N)　　custom, practice
2. 坐月子　　zuò yuèzi　　(VO)　 to be confined to one's house for the month after childbirth
3. 很久以来　hěn jiǔ yǐ lái　(PH)　for a long time now (starting from a certain time in the past)
4. 理解　　　lǐjiě　　　　　(V)　　to understand, to comprehend
* 解　　　　jiě　　　　　　　　　 to explain; to solve (problems); to understand; to unfasten, untie
5. 整整　　　zhěngzhěng　(A)　　whole, full, entire [also: exactly]
6. 补身体　　bǔ shēntǐ　　(VO)　 to nourish one's body (i.e. to restore one's health by eating nutritious food)
7. 中药　　　zhōng yào　　(N)　　Chinese herbal medicine
8. 洗头　　　xǐ-tóu　　　　(VO)　 to wash (one's) hair
9. 紧　　　　jǐn　　　　　(SV/A)　tight, taut / tightly
10. 个子　　 gèzi　　　　　(N)　　physical size of a person, build
* 求　　　　qiú　　　　　　　　　 to plead for, beg for, pray for
* 疼　　　　téng　　　　　　　　　to ache, be painful; be fond of
* 敢　　　　gǎn　　　　　　　　　 to dare (to); bold, courageous
11.* 娶　　　qǔ　　　　　　(V)　　(of a man) to take a wife
* 朵　　　　duǒ　　　　　　　　　 a flower; the lobe of the ear
12. 和……有关 hé ... yǒu guān　　　related to ..., connected with ...

13.	重视	zhòngshì	(SV)	to regard as important
*	视	shì		to consider or regard as; to look at, to see
14.	时代	shídài	(N)	age, era
15.	男女平等	nánnǚpíngděng	(PH)	equality of the sexes
16.	现代	xiàndài	(BF)	modern, contemporary
	现代化	xiàndàihuà	(SV)	modern

第十二章 中秋节——赏月和月饼

"好大好圆的月亮啊！"这是中秋节最美丽的风景了。每年中国农历的八月十五就是中秋节。很多人都知道，中国农历是用月亮的变化来计算的，每个月的十五日就是月圆的时候。所以，每年到了八月十五的时候，大家都会觉得月亮特别的圆、特别的大。家家户户都会在这天晚上准备许多好吃的月饼和水果，一家人坐在外面，一起赏月，一起说话，小朋友们更是忙着玩自己的东西。

除了前面介绍过的春节和端午节以外，中秋节也是一个非常重要的节日。这一天，很多在外面工作的人，都要回到家和家人在一起，因为中国有一句话说：天上的月亮圆，地上的家人全。一个家庭里的每个人都很重要，少了一个人，就不完全了。

大家认为中秋节这一天就是月亮的生日，关于这种说法有一些古老的故事。有一个故事说，在很久很久以前，有一个女神，她的丈夫很有力气。那时候，天上出现了十个太阳，天气很热很热，许多树木、动物和人都被热死了，地上都没有水喝，人们快活不下去了。这时候，女神的丈夫来了，他把九个太阳都打了下来，天上只剩下了一个太阳。从此以后，天气变得不冷不热，人们的生活又开始好起来了。大家都很感谢他，所以决定让他做国王。

可是，女神的丈夫当上国王以后，就变得越来越坏。他一直吃喝玩乐，不管人民的事情，不高兴的时候就随便杀人，他还觉得人民应该永远感谢他。于是，人们的生活又像以前一样痛苦了。有一天，这个国王得到了一种神奇的药，听说吃了这种药，就永远不会死了。老百姓知道了这件事后都很害怕，因为如果国王一直活着，他们的日子就永远不会好过了。

这时候女神知道了人们的想法。有一天女神趁国王不在家的时候，就去把药拿了出来，这时国王刚好回来了，女神一紧张，就把药吃了下去。当她吃了药以后，身体就变得很轻很轻，一下子就飞了起来，一直往天上飞去。国王看见了很生气，就对着她大喊："回来！回来！"

天上的神不喜欢这个突然飞来的女神，因为他们觉得她不应该随便拿别人的东西。女神知道自己不能和其他的神住在天上，只好飞到月亮上去住。几千年以来，中国人一直相信月亮上真的住着一个女神，每年到了中秋节，大家就会拜月亮，感谢她救了大家。

女神并不是一个人住在月亮上的，传说还有一只小白兔和她在一起。如果你用心看月亮，就会发现月亮里有一点黑黑的东西,中国人认为那就是小白兔的眼睛。小白兔在那里每天晚上都努力工作,到了白天才休息。古时候的人说,今天人们的幸福生活都是小白兔晚上辛苦的工作带来的。

中秋节的时候,大家都会吃一种东西,叫做"月饼"。月饼圆圆的,有大的也有小的,里面包了各种馅,非常好吃。每到这一天,大家都会买月饼送给亲人和好朋友,而且卖月饼的人最高兴,因为每年的这个时候生意都非常好。有的人收到月饼,又怕吃不完,就把月饼再送给别人,这样,你送给我月饼,我送给你月饼,有的人收到的月饼就是他前几天送给别人的呢!

每年春季,农民们从早到晚辛苦地种田,每天都不休息,大家都希望种的东西可以快快长大,秋天有个好收获。到了秋天,每个人看到种的东西长得又多又好,心里真的很高兴,因为冬天就不怕没有东西吃了。所以到了中秋节,每个人的心情都很好,看到月亮的时候,也就觉得它更大更圆了。

中秋节的晚上,全家人在院子里聊天、讲故事。晚风轻轻地吹来,天上的星星很美,这时候大家一起吃着月饼、看着月亮,这真是人生中最快乐的事了。

问题

1. 中秋节在每年的什么时候？
2. 中秋节的时候，全家人在一起做什么？
3. 大家为什么让女神的丈夫当国王？
4. 女神为什么会飞到月亮上去？
5. 中秋节的时候，大家都吃什么东西？
6. 中秋节最快乐的事是什么？

生词

1. 赏月　　shǎng-yuè　　(VO)　　to enjoy the moonlight
* 赏　　　shǎng　　　　　　　　to appreciate, enjoy;
　　　　　　　　　　　　　　　　to bestow, to grant, to reward
2. 女神　　nǚshén　　　(N)　　goddess
* 神　　　shén　　　　　　　　god, divine, supernatural
3. 剩下　　shèngxia　　(V)　　to be left over, remainder
* 剩　　　shèng　　　　　　　　to be left over, residue, in excess
4. 从此以后　cóng cǐ yǐhòu　　　from this time on, from now on
* 此　　　cǐ　　　　　　　　　this, these;　such, thus
5. 吃喝玩乐　chī hē wán lè　(PH)　to eat, drink and be merry
6. 痛苦　　tòngkǔ　　(SV/N)　to be painful; suffering, anguish
* 痛　　　tòng　　　　　　　　pain, aching; sorrowful, sad, bitter;
　　　　　　　　　　　　　　　　heartily, to one's heart's content
7. 神奇　　shénqí　　　(SV)　　wondrous, mysterious
8. 老百姓　lǎobǎixìng　(N)　　the (common) people
　　　　　　　　　　　　　　　　(as opposed to the rulers)
9. 突然　　tūrán　　　(A)　　suddenly, unexpectedly
* 突　　　tū　　　　　　　　　abrupt, sudden;　to jut out;
　　　　　　　　　　　　　　　　a break through
10. 以来　　yǐlái　　　　　　　since (a point of time in the past)
11. 拜（拜）bài(bai)　　(V)　　to worship
12.* 救　　jiù　　　　(V)　　to save, to deliver, to rescue

13.	白兔	bái tù	(N)	white rabbit (M: 只)
	兔子	tùzi	(N)	rabbit, hare
*	兔	tù		rabbit, hare
14.	收获	shōuhuò	(V)	to harvest, to reap
			(N)	harvest; fruit (of one's efforts)
*	获	huò		to get, obtain, reap, capture
15.	星星	xīngxing	(N)	stars

第十三章　生日饭和新生儿的名字

虽然每个人都有去世的一天，但是中国人还是希望能活得久一些、好一些。因为这样，就可以做很多想做的事，生活也就会更快乐。从古到今，大家都希望能找到长寿的秘诀。

听说以前中国有一种药，吃了以后，人就不会死了，而且不会老，也不会生病，所以大家都想得到这种药。可是世界上是不是真的有这种药呢？没有人知道，也没有人见过。不过，在中国有另一种方法，听说可以让人活得久一点，这种方法就是吃生日饭。

生日的这一天，过生日的这个人最重要，所以大家都希望他快快乐乐地过生日。家人就会做很多好吃的东西，有时候也会请一些好朋友一起吃。以前，如果过生日的是个小男孩，有的家里除了请客，还会买很多礼物送给他；不过如果是个小女孩，大家就会觉得不那么重要了。

过生日的时候，有一种很特别的面。这种面又细又长，听说吃了这种面的人，他就会活得很长，中国人把这种面叫做"长寿面"。长寿在中国是一件很大很有福气的事情，如果过生日的那个人已经很老了，去吃生日饭的人就会说很多恭喜的话，比如说"祝您寿比南山，福如东海"，老人听了就会很高兴，也会很感谢大家来给他过生日。

中国人希望活得久，也希望活得好。老人要过大寿，小孩子一出生就要有一个好名字。中国人认为名字好，孩子以后的一生都会很好。中国是一个以家庭为中心的社会，小孩子一出生，就要姓爸爸的姓，可是他们的名字就要好好地想一想了。所以在出生前，爸爸妈妈、爷爷奶奶就已经在想小孩的名字了。

如果是男孩，大家就希望他有福气，所以男孩的名字里常常有"福"这个字；如果是女孩，大家就希望她长得好看，所以女孩的名字里常常就有"美"这个字。大家都希望小孩就像他们的名字一样美好。不过古时候，如果小孩出生后身体不好，家人就会故意给孩子起一个很难听的名字。因为听说名字越难听，小孩就越容易养大，就像一些没有名字的小草一样，不去管它，它也能活得很好。

因为中国人比较重男轻女，所以大家都希望生男孩。如果生了女孩，她们的名字里就常常会有"弟弟快来"的意思，比如"招弟"或者"连兄"，意思是希望妈妈下次生男孩。以前在中国女孩子是很没有地位的，因为大家觉得生女孩对家里一点用也没有，而且女孩长大后和别人结了婚，也就是别人家的人了。

中国人认为一个人要活得好，名字一定要好。所以家人想好了孩子的名字以后，还要请有学问的人来看看这个名字好不好：如果以前有同样名字的人活得很好，这个名字就是好名字；如果以前有同样名字的人活得不好，这个名字就不是好名字。所以，给新生儿起一个好名字真是一件不容易的事。

吃生日饭是希望能活得久，给新生儿起个好名字是希望能过得好。中国人这样做，看起来有点好笑，不过在中国，这样做真的会有一些帮助。因为吃生日饭，可以使每个人过生日的时候都很高兴；多听一些好话，心里就会往好的方面想，生活也就会有新的希望；多吃一些好东西，身体就会更好。一个人心情好、身体好，不就可以活得更久一点吗？

　　每个人都想有一个好名字，也喜欢有好名字的人。因为家人和朋友叫他名字时候，他就会想起他名字里的意思。慢慢的，他就记住了名字的意思，这些意思就让他一生常常想起爸爸妈妈对他的希望，这样，一个好名字就真的能帮助一个人认真努力地生活，生活也就会过得很好了。一些特别的中国文化习惯，常常是有道理的，不过这些文化习惯还是以男人为主的。因为在中国，男人一直比女人重要，男人得到的总是比女人多，当然社会也就希望男人做的事更多一些。

问题

1. 过生日时，为什么要吃长寿面？
2. 如果你去吃生日饭，你会说什么祝福的话呢？
3. 为什么男孩的名字里常有"福"这个字，女孩的名字里常有"美"这个字？
4. 你从哪些事情里知道，中国人喜欢儿子而比较不喜欢女儿呢？
5. 一个好名字很重要吗？

生 词

1. 新生儿　xīnshēng'ér　(N)　newborn child
2. 长寿　chángshòu　(N)　longevity, a long life
* 寿　shòu　　longevity, old age; the life span
3. 秘诀　mìjué　(N)　the secret (e.g. of success)
* 秘　mì　　secret, confidential; mysterious
* 诀　jué　　knack; sorcery; to part, separate
* 海　hǎi　　sea, ocean
4. 一生　yìshēng　(N)　whole life, a lifetime
5. 起名字　qǐ míngzi　(VO)　to name, to give a name to ... (or 取名字)
6. 难听　nántīng　(SV)　unpleasant to listen to, to grate on the ears
7. 管　guǎn　(V)　to pay heed to, pay attention to
8. 重男轻女　zhòngnánqīngnǚ　(PH)　to regard males more highly than females, male supremacy
* 兄　xiōng　　elder brother; term of respect used in addressing a senior of the same generation
9. 同样　tóngyàng　(A)　alike, similar [or in the same way/manner]
* 总　zǒng　　always; chief, principal, central; all, overall, general

PATTERN

| 以……为…… | to take/regard ... as ... |
| 以男人为主 | to regard men as the more important (of the sexes) |

第十四章　重阳节

中秋节过了以后，天气慢慢变凉了。中国农历的七月、八月和九月都是秋季，九月到了，秋天也快要过去了。这个时候天气会变得更凉更冷，有时候还会下雪呢！每年的这个时候，如果天气好，有时间的话，人们就会到外面去玩，因为以后的天气会越来越冷，就不能再出去了。中国农历九月有一个节日，叫做"重阳节"。

"重阳节"在每年的九月九日。中国人很喜欢"九"这个数字，因为"九"和"久"的读音是一样的，"九九"听起来就像"久久"，有长久平安的意思。在中国，一个能活得很久的人，就是有福气的人。所以，九月九日也是中国的老人节。大家都希望自己的父母和年老的亲人能活得很久，一直到九十九岁。在这一天，大家都会送老人一些很好的东西，希望他们能活得更久，生活得更快乐。

以前到了重阳节这一天，人们都会带着好吃的东西，换上舒服的衣服，到比较高的地方去，因为他们相信比较高的地方离天上的神很近，神也能听到他们说的话。

但是关于重阳节，还有这样一个古老的传说。有一年，中秋节过后的一天，天上的神对一位年轻人说："你家附近会发生一件大事，就是在九月九日的那一天，那里所有的人和动物都会死，除非你们在那天跑到山上去，同时要喝菊花酒，这样，死亡和不好的事就不会发生在你们身上了。"

那位年轻人听了这话，就跑回去告诉他的家人和附近的亲人、朋友。于是他们在九月九日那天，都离开了家，爬到山上去了。后来等他们回来的时候，看见许多没有离开家的人和动物都已经死了。从那以后，人们在九月九日这一天，就会到山上去，这一天也成了中国人的一个文化节日。

现在每年的重阳节，许多家庭都会带着小孩子一起去爬山，这已经成了一个很有意义的家庭活动。爬山的时候，大家走走停停，走累了，就停下来休息休息。休息的时候，大家可以坐在路边吃吃东西、喝喝水。休息够了以后，再继续往上爬。

秋天的天气是最舒服的，上山虽然有一点累，但是每个人都觉得很快乐。到了山上，空气非常好，每个人的心情也都特别好，就这样，大家慢慢地走到了最高的地方。

到了山上一看，已经有很多人在那里了。山上到处都是菊花，有黄色的，也有白色的，各种颜色的菊花在一起非常漂亮。菊花是一种不怕冷的花，虽然天气越来越冷，它还是会开得很漂亮。所以从过去到现在，中国人都很喜欢菊花，而且画画的时候，很多人也都喜欢画菊花。

重阳节的时候，很多地方都有"菊花大会"。这时候，各种菊花都会被放在一起，就像菊花海一样。有的人为菊花作诗；有的人为菊花作画；有的人忙着卖菊花或者买菊花；还有许多人在认真地欣赏菊花；小孩子到处跑。各种声音一会儿高一会儿低，到处都是人，非常热闹。

菊花不只是好看，还可以拿来吃。重阳节的时候，大家都会喝菊花茶，或者菊花酒。中国人认为，菊花是一种药，听说喝了菊花茶或者菊花酒以后，身体会变得很健康，而且菊花茶和菊花酒对眼睛也很好。菊花的好处这么多，所以中国人才会这么喜欢菊花。

从山上往下看，可以看到很远的地方。山下的房子都变得很小。在这个时候，每个人都会觉得自己在这个世界上很小。以前，有一个很有名的诗人，他在重阳节的时候，从高处往下看，写下了一首想念家人的诗。后来每年到了重阳节，大家都会想起他的诗，心里也同样会想起亲人和朋友。

现在的重阳节已经没有菊花大会了，到山上去的人也不像以前那么多了。可是，重阳节这一天，大家还是会想起家人，想起年长的老人。有的人做完工作后，会快一点回到家里看看年老的父母；有些人虽然不能回家，还是会打电话、写信回家，问问父母最近好不好。从古到今，中国人孝顺的心一直没有改变。

问题

1. 中国农历的九月天气怎么样？
2. 中国的老人节为什么要在九月九日？
3. 重阳节时，为什么要到高的地方去？
4. "菊花大会"里有些什么东西？
5. 菊花有什么用处？

生词

1.	重阳节	Chóngyángjié	(N)	Double Ninth Festival
*	凉	liáng		cool, chilly
*	雪	xuě		snow
2.	数字	shùzì	(N)	numeral, figure, digit
3.	读音	dúyīn	(N)	pronunciation (of a word)
4.	长久	chángjiǔ	(TW)	a very long time
*	附	fù		near or close to; to rely on; to attach or enclose; to add to
5.	菊花	júhuā	(N)	chrysanthemum (flower)
*	菊	jú		chrysanthemum
6.	死亡	sǐwáng	(N/V)	death / to die
*	亡	wáng		dead; to perish; to flee
7.	有意义	yǒu yìyì	(SV)	meaningful, significant
*	义	yì		righteousness, justice; charity, generosity; meaning
8.	大会	dàhuì	(N)	conference, rally, large meeting
9.	欣赏	xīnshǎng	(V)	to enjoy, appreciate (e.g. a view)
*	欣	xīn		glad(ly), joyful(ly), delighted
*	首	shǒu		Measure for songs & poems; the first, beginning; leader, chief
10.	年长	niánzhǎng	(SV)	older in age, senior

11. 用处   yòngchu   (N)   use or purpose (to which an object may be employed)

第十五章　汉字的故事

很久很久以前，人们是先会说话，然后才会写字的。在文字还没发明以前，大家说完话以后，很快就忘记说了些什么，所以，常常有人忘记做事情，也有人做完以后忘记做了什么事情。于是，古人们都想找一些方法把说过的话、做过的事记下来。

刚开始有人想到用绳子打结的方法来记事。发生了一件事就打一个结，发生了两件事就打两个结。慢慢的，事情越来越多，打的结也越来越多，最后大家还是把事情忘记了。后来又有人用画画来记事：有的人画在土上，过了几天，下了雨，画就不见了；有的人画在树上，可是树圆圆的，很难画上去，而且，也不能把树带走，实在不方便！

古人们想来想去，看到房子旁边的地上有很多骨头，那些骨头都是他们吃肉剩下的。他们找了找，找到了一些表面比较平的骨头，就把画刻在了骨头上。结果他们发现这个方法很不错，这样，中国字就开始出现了。几千年以后，人们在地下找到了很多这样的骨头，上面都刻着一些奇怪的图画，那都是古时候的人写的字，中国人把它们叫做"甲骨文"。

古时候的人是怎么用图画来记事的呢？比方说，那时候，有人看到了太阳，就画了一个⊙。他说太阳是圆的，中间有一点黑，大家都觉得他说的很对，以后，大家看到这个画就知道它是太阳的意思。从那以后，古人们就用图画把很多事情记了下来，也用图画把要说的意思告诉了别人和后来的人。

你看，"月"这个字看起来真有点像天上的月亮呢！"木"这个字看起来也很像一棵树。有很多汉字看起来很像真的东西，但是有一些人觉得画画太麻烦，就把画写成比较简单的记号或符号了。后来，人们又觉得，汉字虽然很好，很方便，可是有很多意思还是没有办法写出来。于是，中国人又开始想办法了，他们用原来的字又发明了新的字。比如，"明"这个字是很亮的意思，世界上什么东西最亮呢？当然是太阳和月亮，把一个"日"和一个"月"放在一起，就很明亮了，所以"明"字就是这样来的。从古时候到现在，经过很长时间的变化，这些字就变成了今天我们所熟悉的"汉字"。

有的时候一个汉字可以表示一个意思，比如"天"、"地"。但有的时候，需要两个字才能表示一个意思，像"大家"、"东西"，如果把两个字分开，就没有原来的意思了。还有用三个字或者四个字来表示一个意思的，比方说"说一不二"，意思是说了什么话就应该不变，要不然以后别人就会不相信你了。像这样四个字在一起的词，中国人叫做"成语"。成语可以帮助人们用简单的四个字，把复杂的意思简单地说明白。

汉字里的同音字也很多，像"是"、"事"、"市"，它们的发音都一样，所以汉语里有很多说法都是和字音有关的。比如，如果你去中国人家里的时候，千万要记得送东西不可以送钟，为什么不能送钟呢？因为"送钟"和"送终"的发音是一样的，如果你送的是钟，就好像希望别人快点死，他们会很不高兴的。

从古到今，汉字的用法也一直在变化。如果把古时候的人写的东西拿来看，很多的人已经看不懂了。古时候的人写的东西，我们叫做"古文"。但是到了现在，写字、说话和古时候完全不一样了。所以现在的人就看不太懂古文了。也许再过几百年，以后的人也看不懂我们现在的文字了。

汉字除了可以记事以外，中国人还常常把它当画来画。以前很多有名的人，他们写的字都像画一样好看。有的读书人还把写字当作一生的工作。如果他的字写得好，就会有人买下来，放在家里欣赏，除了看字的意思，也要看字的样子。汉字如果写得好，就像图画一样美丽。中国人把这种艺术叫做"书法"。

看了汉字的这些故事，你还会觉得汉字难吗？从汉字的历史里，人们可以知道很多有意思的事情。英文不是有一句话说："Practice makes perfect"。学习写汉字也是一样的道理，中国有一个成语叫"熟能生巧"，所以多多练习，你的汉字就会越写越好。

问题

1. 以前的人用过哪些记事方法？
2. 现在的汉字是怎样变来的？
3. "明"字和"日"、"月"有什么关系？
4. 什么是成语？成语有什么用处？
5. 送礼(物)时，为什么不能送钟？
6. 现在的人看得懂古文吗？ 为什么？
7. 怎样才能写好汉字？

生 词

1.	文字	wénzì	(N)	written language
2.	绳子	shéngzi	(N)	rope
*	绳	shéng		rope, cord; to rectify, to correct
3.	打结	dǎ-jié	(VO)	to tie a knot
4.	骨头	gǔtou	(N)	bone
*	骨	gǔ		bone; framework, skeleton
5.	表面	biǎomiàn	(N)	on the surface
6.	平	píng	(SV)	flat, even (surface)
7.*	刻	kè	(V)	to carve, engrave; quarter of an hour; cruel, heartless
8.	甲骨文	jiǎgǔwén	(N)	oracle bone writings
*	甲	jiǎ		armor, shell, crust; 1st of the 10 Celestial Stems
9.	中间	zhōngjiān	(PW)	(in) the middle/center
*	棵	kē		Measure for trees
10.	记号	jìhào	(N)	a mark, a sign
11.	符号	fúhào	(N)	a symbol, a sign
*	符	fú		an identification tag or label; an omen; a charm; to tally
*	熟	shú		very familiar; (of fruit) ripe; (of food) cooked, well-done
*	悉	xī		to know; all, total, entire

*	词	cí		words, phrases, expressions
12.	成语	chéngyǔ	(N)	4-character idiom or saying
*	复	fù		complex; double, overlapping; to repeat; to answer, reply to recover, to return to normal
*	杂	zá		miscellaneous; to mix, to blend
13.	同音	tóngyīn	(N)	the same tone, a homophone
14.	字音	zìyīn	(N)	pronunciation of a character
15.	钟	zhōng	(N)	a clock
16.	送终	sòng-zhōng	(VO)	to prepare for the burial of one's parents
*	终	zhōng		to come to the end, conclusion; finally, at last; death, pass away
17.	古文	gǔwén	(N)	ancient style of Chinese writing
18.	读书人	dúshūrén	(N)	a person of learning, a scholar
19.	艺术	yìshù	(N)	art
*	艺	yì		art, skill, talent
*	术	shù		a skill, a feat; way or method
*	巧	qiǎo		ingenious, skillful; a clever feat; coincidence
*	系	xì		relationship; college/university department; a system

ENGLISH TRANSLATION OF THE STORIES

Chapter 1 Spring Festival — Red Envelopes and the New Year's Eve Meal

The Spring Festival is China's most important festival. Why is it called "Spring Festival"? The meaning of "Spring Festival" is that winter is almost over and spring is just about to arrive, i.e. another year is almost over and a new year is just about to begin. As one year follows another, celebrating the Spring Festival is also called "Celebrating the (New) Year".

Every Chinese person will tell you that celebrating the New Year is very important. Every year at this time, the whole family will happily gather together. After the New Year celebrations are over, everyone hopes for a good and new beginning.

In order to welcome in a new year, in the period just before the Spring Festival, each family and household are all very busy. The most important chore is to clean the house and put everything in order. The house has to be thoroughly cleaned inside and out, so everyone is busy tidying up their own things— the adults are busy and so are the children. The few days before Spring Festival, no matter whether male or female, everyone is busy preparing for the New Year. Some put the rooms in order, some tidy up the yard. Every family is so busy. Everybody likes a clean house ready for celebrating the Spring Festival, don't they?

There is another big task the families will be busy doing before the Spring Festival, that is, buying things for the New Year celebrations. There are many things one needs for the New Year celebrations — food, clothes, firecrackers, light refreshments, wine, etc. are all needed for the Spring Festival. It is very important to buy these things, because during the Spring Festival almost everyone is at home resting and almost all the stores don't open. So you must definitely buy lots of things in order to be well prepared.

When the house is clean and the shopping for the Spring Festival has been done, this is the time when everyone is busy preparing to celebrate the Spring Festival. The men are busy writing the New Year couplets, and the women are busy preparing the New Year's Eve meal. The elderly are busy preparing new clothes, and the children are busy preparing the firecrackers they will want to play with. New Year couplets are two pieces of long red paper. They have good wishes for the New Year written on them. Chinese people like red color most of all, so therefore writing pleasing words on red paper is even better. After writing the couplets, people paste them on each side of their front door, so during the New Year celebrations everyone can see all the main doors hung with bright red couplets, which is extremely pretty.

Sometimes Chinese people write the character "福" on a piece of red paper and paste it on their front door. However, they often paste the character "福" upside down on purpose. Those who don't know this custom will say: "'福' is upside down! '福' is upside down!" ("Fu dao le!"), which sounds just like; "The blessing has arrived! The blessing has arrived!" ("Fu dao le!") Whenever people hear these kinds of sayings, they feel even happier!

Chinese people call the day before the Spring Festival "Year 30", and the evening of "Year 30" is called "New Year's Eve". In the morning of "Year 30", the women get up very early to prepare the New Year's Eve meal, because New Year's Eve is the most important time of the whole Spring Festival. In ancient times, transportation in China was very inconvenient; if a member of the family was far away from home studying or doing business, it was not at all easy for them to return home. However, no matter how far away they were, for New Year's Eve, everyone in other parts (of China) must drop everything and return home to be with their families to eat the New Year's Eve meal, because in Chinese people's minds, home is the most important place.

In the past, the New Year's Eve meal was the most important meal of the year, and possibly the most sumptuous one, because in those days, Chinese people's living conditions weren't very good, and so it was only at Chinese New Year that many families could eat chicken, duck, fish and meat. Nowadays life is much better for Chinese people, and people can regularly eat lots of delicious food, but the New Year's Eve meal is still the most important meal of the year. Because after returning to one's own home, and seeing one's family members again, everyone is eating the New Year's Eve meal while talking and laughing together, so all the weariness and unhappiness of the past year is forgotten, so eating the New Year's Eve meal is the happiest time of year for Chinese people.

Many other fun things happen on New Year's Eve. After the New Year's Eve meal is over, the children wait to be given their red packets by the adults. A "red packet" is a red-colored paper envelope where some money has been put into it by someone and used as a present for relatives and friends. The children say some nice New Year-related sayings to the adults, and the adults give them red packets. A wish the adults love to hear most is: "Happy New Year!" Children like this time each year best of all, because when they have received the red packets, they can go and buy the things they like, for example firecrackers and toys.

In the evening of "Year 30" (New Year's Eve), although everyone is a little tired, nobody wants to go to bed. Everyone wants to wait until midnight to await the arrival of the New Year. At twelve o'clock sharp, each home sets off firecrackers at the same time. The New Year has arrived! Everybody is one year older!

The next day, which is the first day of the New Year, everybody wears new clothes. The first words expressed to people seen in the New Year are: "Good New Year!" Everyone hopes that it will get off to a good start. The adults take the children to visit relatives and friends. Although the children don't necessarily want to go, they know that if they do go, they might receive red packets — this is what they hope for!

The Spring Festival has gone by happily and quickly. Everyone goes back to their normal lives again. Working people begin work again, students will start to study. The Spring Festival is a new beginning. Everyone hopes that this year will be even better than last year. Adults hope that they can make even more money in the new year, and of course many children hope to get even more red packets next Spring Festival!

Chapter 2 The Lantern Festival — Viewing Lanterns and Eating Sweet Dumplings

The 15th day after the lunar New Year is "Lantern Festival" and is the first major festival of the new year. Each year on this day the moon in the sky is both large and round, and this is the first full moon of the new year. Even though the weather in many places is still cold at this time (of year), yet people's hearts are warm and happy because they see the beautiful moon in the sky.

There are 15 days between the Spring Festival and the Lantern Festival. This equals the period of the New Year Celebration. It is only after the Lantern Festival is over that all the excitement of the New Year (celebrations) will slowly come to an end, so the Lantern Festival is the final day of the Spring Festival. On this day many places are still bustling with noise and activity; some places have singing, some places have dancing and some other places have many interesting activities. People are as happy as during the New Year celebrations and everyone wants to continue having fun right into the evening.

In ancient times it wasn't that easy to go out at night because, in those days, there were no electric lights. Everyone went home as soon as the sun set and generally didn't go out in the evening. If someone didn't come home after dark, their family members would worry. But because the Lantern Festival is the last day of the Spring Festival, so everyone hopes to be able to go outside for a walk.

Legend has it that in ancient times there was an emperor who considered the Lantern Festival to be a very special festival. He thought that the moon that night was particularly bright and beautiful, so if everyone could go out for a walk and look (at the moon), wouldn't this be a good thing? So the emperor allowed all his citizens to go out on that night. From that time on, every year on the night of the Lantern Festival everyone goes outdoors to enjoy themselves.

Although the moon shines brightly on the evening of the Lantern Festival, it is still comparatively dark outside. In order to allow everyone to be able to see clearly, lanterns are hung in front of all the houses. Some rich homes in particular hang up many large lanterns so that the night becomes as bright as the day. Many people walking in the streets carry lanterns in their hands, so in this way, in the sky there's a large moon, on earth there are thousands of lanterns! Everyone loves to come out on this evening, because there are lanterns everywhere, so this holiday is also called "Lantern Festival". [Note: In Chinese there are two names for it: Yuan Xiao Festival and Deng Festival]

In the evening of the Lantern Festival, everyone will go to the temple (courtyard) to view the lanterns. There will be many lanterns of every sort and kind there hung in front of the temple. All these lanterns are hand-made, large ones and small ones, and are extremely beautiful to look at. In ancient times the lanterns were all made of paper and often painted with pretty designs. When looking at these beautiful lanterns, people's eyes started to shine.

There are often activities in front of the temple to make the Lantern Festival even livelier, (such as) singing and dancing, etc. Also there is one special activity at Lantern Festival: people ask interesting questions (= riddles) for others to guess (the answer). If a person guesses right, he is given a present for guessing the riddle correctly, so the people who ask the questions are delighted and so are those who are guessing, as well as those looking at all the fun.

Very often these riddles are written on the paper of the lanterns and as people view the lanterns they also read the riddles and try to guess the answers. This activity only happens during the Lantern Festival, and we call this "Guessing the Riddle on the Lantern".

Here is an example of an old riddle: What has four legs when it is born, becomes two legs when it is grown up, and becomes three legs when it is old? Can you guess what this is? The answer is: man. When a person is just born, he uses his hands and feet to crawl on the ground; after he has grown up, he walks on two legs; when he is old, he needs a stick to help him walk which makes it look like he is (walking on) three legs. Did you guess correctly? During the Lantern Festival, people will often ask many of this kind of interesting riddles.

Young and old will go out to have fun during the Lantern Festival. The adults like to look at the lanterns while chatting with other people. Many of the children happily run back and forth carrying their own hand-made lanterns. Seen from afar, the lanterns they are carrying look like a living golden dragon, flying this way and that. It's really interesting!

Many young unmarried men and women will also go out on this occasion for a fun time. Everyone is dressed in beautiful clothes and is out viewing the lanterns, also taking the opportunity to make many (new) friends. However, in ancient China, boys were usually together with boys and the girls were together with girls. The culture at that time was for boys and girls not to walk too closely together.

Besides looking at the moon and viewing the lanterns, on this day every household will eat Yuan Xiao (= a special kind of small sweet dumpling). The sweet dumplings are round and white, just like the round moon in the sky. In China, the sweet dumplings made in the north are not the same as those in the south. But one thing is the same, (the meaning behind) eating Yuan Xiao is that everyone hopes that the days will be good ones in the new year (just begun), and hopes that all the family members can normally be together.

After the wonderful Lantern Festival celebrations are over, a new year begins. In order to have a happy life, everyone ought to work hard. Those who work get ready to go out to work, business men get ready to start doing business again, and students prepare to go back to school to start studying again. The spring breeze gently starts to blow and the flowers begin to bloom. From now on, everybody will start to be busy again!

Chapter 3 Marriage—the Matchmaker and the Wedding Banquet

If a man loves a woman, and at the same time the woman also loves that man, can they get married? In ancient China this would not have been easy and many times it would not be allowed because in those days a person's marriage was decided by their parents. All their lives, a girl was not allowed to go out just whenever she pleased, so there weren't many opportunities for girls to get to know boys. After the 16th birthday, their parents would start looking for a suitable partner for them. Sometimes the child wasn't even born yet but the parents had already decided whom he/she ought later to marry.

Social status used to be the most important conditional factor in marriage. Everyone hoped to find a partner who was of the same social status to be married to. Wealthy people looked for wealthy people to marry; poor people looked for poor people to marry, because they believed that, only if the two people had the same social status, after they got married would they be truly happy. But how can one go about finding someone with the same social status? Many times people needed the help of someone, and this person is the "matchmaker".

In China, the matchmaker is normally a woman who is already married, and knows many people. If somebody is thinking of getting married, they would ask the matchmaker for help. The matchmaker's job was to introduce a boy to a girl to get acquainted with each other and help them get married.

Before the two of them get married, they don't know each other, so how to get these two unacquainted people married? At this point in time, one needs the matchmaker to come forward and put in a good word for both sides.

At first the boy's family will ask the matchmaker to go to the girl's home to see the girl and her family, and ask the girl's side if they would like her to marry the boy. Sometimes the matchmaker asked the boy's family's opinion and sometimes she helped the girl's family come up with some ideas, so in order to help these two people get married, she was busy every day. Her biggest wish was that the two would be able to get married. If they did get married, the two families will be very grateful to her. Being a matchmaker isn't just a job, it also means helping others!

If the girl's family agreed to the marriage, the matchmaker would have lots to do, and would also have to pay careful attention to many details. In this way, no problems would arise at the wedding. At first the man's family will ask the matchmaker to deliver some presents to the girl's home. If the girl's family accepted these gifts, the wedding would almost certainly take place. If the girl's family did not accept the gifts, there were possibly still some problems with the marriage arrangements.

After this, the man's family will go to the woman's family. This time is when the man's family will really discuss the issues of marriage and the man's family will give the woman's family money and an extremely nice gift. If her family accept these, the marriage is set. After the man's family has returned home, they will decide on a wedding date and matters concerning which guests to invite. The man's family and the woman's family both hope for the wedding date to soon arrive. For the couple and their families, the wedding is a large happy event, so the day of the wedding will be very lively. The man getting married is called the bridegroom, and the woman getting married is called the bride. On the (wedding) day itself, the groom takes a few people with him to collect the bride. They pick her up at her home and bring her back to his home. The bride is dressed in the most beautiful red clothes and her heart is both happy and sad: happy because she is about to be married, but sad because she will leave her parents. For this reason the bride will both cry and laugh on her wedding day. Everyone knows how she feels and so nobody thinks it strange.

When the bride and groom get married, many people will come to see the bride. On this day she is the most beautiful of all. However, if too many people come to look at the bride, she will be very embarrassed. In ancient times brides wore a piece of red cloth over their heads (like a veil) so as not to allow others to see her face. Even though everyone could not see the bride's face, they were happy (just) to be able to see her.

Everybody has to pay careful attention to many things at this time: one is not permitted (to say and do) whatever one pleases, (e.g. one's not allowed) to make negative comments or say impolite things or do something everyone considers improper. If something needs to be done at this time, it is best to ask someone who knows, like the mother, grandmother or the matchmaker, because they are very experienced people, and (so) if there is any problem, everyone will ask them their opinion.

The two families getting married will invite their relatives and friends to the wedding banquet. (The purpose of) the wedding banquet is to invite everyone for a meal. On this occasion, you can eat the most delicious dishes and drink the best wine. Everybody has a wonderful time talking and laughing together. The two families also have this added opportunity to get to know one another better. Everybody drinks with the bride and groom and hopes that they will be together forever. They also hope that they will soon give birth and have many children, because Chinese people consider that having lots of children is (a symbol of) happiness and good fortune.

In the evening, the groom is still outside drinking with many people; by this time the bride has already gone back into their room to wait for her husband. She has to keep the red veil on her head until the groom comes in to remove it. After the banquet, many friends will go to the bride and groom's bedroom and play jokes on the couple in any way possible. They tell the couple to do strange things or ask them odd questions. Only after playing all kinds of jokes on them will the friends finally leave. Chinese people call this custom "Disturbing the Bridal Chamber".

The wedding day may be the first time the bride and groom meet. The bridegroom removes the red veil very gently from the bride's head, and the bride feels very embarrassed and lowers her head. No matter what the groom and the bride might look like, they are already husband and wife. After their marriage, the husband will have to work hard and the wife will have to take care of the house. As one day follows the next, the two people really begin to know and love each other.

Chapter 4 Drinking Wine and Drinking Tea

Noodles and rice are the staple diet of Chinese people. Besides these, green vegetables, fruit and meat are also important. However, there are two other things that are necessary to life for Chinese people. If these two things did not exist, life would be very dull and boring. So what are these two things? They are alcohol and tea.

Alcohol and tea play a very important part in Chinese people's social life. They are used on many occasions. Sometimes alcohol and tea are used to remember the dear departed. They also use wine and tea at wedding banquets for congratulating (i.e. toasting) the bride and groom. When friends come for a visit, people especially like to entertain them with alcoholic beverages or tea. With alcohol and tea, life becomes even livelier and more interesting.

There is a long history of Chinese people drinking alcohol. Three to four thousand years ago the Chinese knew how to make wine, so since then Chinese people have enjoyed drinking alcoholic beverages. People often drink a little during their leisure time while chatting and telling jokes. After drinking some wine, people's faces turn really red and their hearts feel very warm. As soon as one is happy, people say whatever is on their mind, so in this way, everyone becomes good friends.

From ancient times right up until the present, many famous people have loved drinking wine. One of these famous historical people was a poet named Li Bai. He liked drinking wine very much. Whenever he drank wine, he wrote even better poems. It is said that he often held his cup up and faced the moon and invited the moon to drink with him. See just how unusual those ancient poets were! This is how Li Bai wrote many fine poems. However, according to legend, Li Bai drank too much and ended up falling into the river and died.

There are many kinds of wine in China and each place produces a different kind of wine. Drinking habits are also not the same. Northerners are more large-hearted and drink in big gulps because they feel that drinking can only be fun if done in this way. However, southerners pay more attention to detail and drink their wine in tiny sips because they believe that only by drinking slowly can it be enjoyable. However, no matter how one drinks, it all finally ends up in one's stomach anyway.

Not only are the drinking habits of southerners and northerners different, each person's drinking habits also differ and their moods when drinking differ greatly. Some people go to find drinking partners when they feel happy (so as) to let people know that they are happy; others go to find drinking partners when they are feeling sad (so as) to let their friends know they are sad; there are also others who go to find drinking partners when they have nothing much to do to let everyone know they have nothing to do. So in this way, you seek me out for a drink or I seek you out for a drink. When people feel like drinking, it isn't difficult to find a reason! However, we all know that drinking too much alcohol is not good for one's health.

Drinking tea is also very popular in China. Chinese people started drinking tea a long time ago. So how did tea-drinking start? One version tells about a man in ancient times who was boiling some water when he saw a few tree leaves fall down into it. The water immediately changed color and became bright yellow as well as having a slight fragrant smell. Because this kind of liquid was made from tree leaves, people called it tea. In the beginning everyone regarded tea as a kind of medicine. In the end, because it tasted so good, people enjoyed drinking tea even when they were not sick. Nowadays there are many people who drink tea almost every day.

There are many varieties of tea: black tea, green tea, Jasmine tea, etc. Some of the teas are grown in winter and others are grown in summer. These different varieties, because they are grown in different seasons, when drinking them they feel quite different. Tea-drinking is an art in China and many people research methods of drinking tea, so in ancient times quite a few people wrote books about tea, and things related to tea are the (main) content of these books. It is obvious that tea is important in China!

When Chinese people drink tea they are usually in quite a good mood and are wanting to relax, because it is important to pay attention to the method and proper time of drinking so that the tea will taste better. No matter whether they are northerners or southerners, everyone takes their time drinking their tea, and furthermore, while drinking tea, people often enjoy eating some tasty light refreshments. Drinking tea, eating light refreshments, and chatting together with good friends — what can be happier than doing this!

Drinking too much alcohol is bad for you. But there are things that need to be observed when drinking tea as well. Firstly, it is best not to drink tea that has been brewed for a long while. We call this kind of tea "old tea". It will become quite bitter and is not good for one's health. Secondly, one cannot drink tea while taking medicine, because tea is a kind of medicine itself, and so can change the other medicine and render it ineffective. So if you drink tea while taking medicine, the medicine will be of no benefit to you. Thirdly, you can drink tea and wine often, but don't drink too much. If you drink too much tea, you might not want to eat your meal.

Actually drinking wine and drinking tea not only make oneself feel good, their biggest benefit is that they are able to bring us constantly together with our friends. Affection between friends can increase greatly when drinking tea or wine. If two people who were originally unacquainted spend time together drinking wine or tea, while chatting they will slowly get to know one another. So if you have a chance to visit Chinese friends, take along a bottle of wine or some good tea for them as this will surely make them very happy.

Note: The word "酒" has a wider meaning in Chinese than in English. It has therefore sometimes been translated as wine and sometimes alcohol.

Chapter 5 Tomb Sweeping Day—the Day for Commemorating One's Ancestors

Everyone knows that a year has four seasons: spring, summer, autumn and winter. However, in ancient times, Chinese people, besides dividing the year into four seasons, also separated it into 24 divisions of the solar year. In this way, each month has two of these divisions. (These) divisions helped ancient people, especially farmers, in being more aware of the changes in weather. The division called Tomb Sweeping Day is also a festival. If we calculate it according to the western method (i.e. calendar), it probably falls just before or after April 5th.

Among the Chinese festivals, Tomb Sweeping Day is one that came into being quite late. It originally was part of the Cold Food Festival. The Cold Food Festival was seven days long and Tomb Sweeping Day took place during the last two days of it. One cannot use fire to cook food during the Cold Food Festival. Tomb Sweeping Day is for paying respects to one's ancestors at their grave. In the end, the Cold Food Festival slowly disappeared and so paying one's respects at one's ancestors' graves on the day of Tomb Sweeping Day turned into an annual tradition as more people got to know about it and accepted it.

It just so happens that Tomb Sweeping Day falls in the spring when the weather is beautiful. The spring sunshine makes people feel warm and comfortable, and all around one can see pretty flowers and grass and green trees. Visiting and sweeping the graves is the most important aspect of Tomb Sweeping Day. The graves are usually up in the mountains. Every family will take lots of things with them when they go to "sweep the graves". People going to visit the graves can be seen everywhere. It is an extremely important day.

What does "sweeping the graves" mean? It is the time each year when all family members go to their ancestors' graves to remember the dear departed. The graves are mostly up in the mountains, and as time goes by, the grass around the graves grows very high. Each year on Tomb Sweeping Day, everyone goes to their ancestor's graves to pull out the weeds and sweep the ground (around the grave) in order to tidy up the cemetery, so (this is why) this day's activity is called "sweeping the graves".

Tomb Sweeping Day is the day on which Chinese remember their dear departed, so sweeping the graves is a way of expressing (loving) remembrance of one's dear ones. When they arrive in the mountains, people will first tidy all the grass up, then place the fruit and all the food they brought with them in front of the grave. Everybody kneels quietly while remembering their dear departed, hoping that they are blissfully happy underground (i.e. in the afterworld) and (the living) wish for a peaceful life for those still on this earth.

Besides bringing food for the dear departed, large sums of paper money are also brought along. It isn't real money – it's fake money, and is used for remembering one's departed relatives. Those who go to "sweep the graves" burn the paper money in front of the grave for the dead to use. Chinese people think that people, after they die, will continue living in the afterworld, so they still need to use money. So paper money is burned in the hope that the ancestors will have money for use in the afterlife. After burning the money, the living (relatives) then express their heartfelt feelings to the dear departed.

Sometimes the relatives who live in other places will also return to pay their respects at the family grave. Normally people are busy in their own job so that it's difficult to have an opportunity to meet up.

When relatives have all come home for Tomb Sweeping Day, everyone has a great opportunity to see each other. After sweeping the grave, everyone sits together to rest and talk about their own family-related matters. Amongst the relatives, some will have grown to be adults as the years have gone by, others just got married last year and this year now have a child. One year follows the next and time goes by quickly. Seeing the number of one's own relatives increasing and life getting better and better, everyone feels happy together, and so everyone thinks that the ancestors who had already passed away will also be happy on this day.

If the weather is really good on the day of Tomb Sweeping Day, after everyone has "swept the graves", they will go to some places for a time of casual fun. For instance, climb a mountain to see the view, or go for a casual stroll, or else with the relatives together for a simple activity. These activities are not because people want to be entertained, but rather to help us think about (the meaning of) life and to understand the beauty of life.

On Tomb Sweeping Day, many people will go out to fly kites. And what is a kite? It is an object made of paper which can fly. Kites have a very long string at the head of it for pulling, so if there is a wind, the kite will fly upwards. People hold onto the string tightly, so in this way the kite won't fly away. The higher the kite flies, the happier people feel!

At this time one can see many pretty kites everywhere in the sky. Many of the kites are made into different animal shapes, and when they are flying in the sky, the sky looks just like a zoo. At this time, lots of people sit on the grass looking at the beautiful view while eating delicious snacks and enjoying themselves tremendously on the grass.

Long, long ago there was a painter who painted a picture. It was a very long Chinese painting, and was painted beautifully. The painting depicts Chinese people on Tomb Sweeping Day doing different activities. Altogether there are over 1600 people and more than 200 animals in the painting. Each person is different: some people are looking at the view, others are buying something. There are also many carts and ships in the painting. We can learn a lot about life in earlier times from this painting.

In south-eastern China, possibly because of geographical reasons or possibly due to climatic reasons, the weather is usually bad on Tomb Sweeping Day and it normally rains. Because in ancient times people couldn't go out to work when it rained, they therefore had a lot of time at home together with their families. Rainy weather seems to reflect people's moods. When it rains, those away from home would think affectionately of their own family members, and would ponder on matters of human life.

Tomb Sweeping Day is a day to remember one's ancestors, and it is also a day of thanksgiving for everyone. Remembering those departed ones and thanking them for all that they had done in the past, because if it weren't for the hard work of those relatives who went before us, life would not be so wonderful today.

(So) Tomb Sweeping Day is the day when the Chinese remember their ancestors.

Chapter 6   Stuffing Dumplings — Inviting Guests to a Lively Feast

Many people say that Chinese culture is a "food" culture. And why do they put it like this? Because Chinese people are not only clever, they also know how to eat well! All that flies in the sky, crawls on the ground and many things that live in the water, they can make every kind into delicious Chinese dishes, so people often say: "The good cuisine is in China." It goes without saying that Chinese cuisine is famous the world over.

However, cooking Chinese food is very troublesome, and one often needs to spend a lot of time at it. If guests come, the host must spend a long time preparing the food and this can be quite tiring. One can also feel that making lots of dishes isn't the most convenient way of going about entertaining people. So a different way of entertaining guests appeared.

This method is both easy and convenient and one doesn't need to spend lots of time or lots of money, and what is even more important is that what one makes tastes delicious. So, what is this method? It is stuffing dumplings. Dumplings were invented by northerners in China. Because the weather in the north of China is colder, there is no rice to eat, (hence) their staple diet are products made from wheat, so northerners make a wide variety of dishes from wheat flour, and dumplings is one of them.

To make dumplings one needs to prepare two things: the dumpling wrapping and the filling for the dumplings. The wrapping for the dumplings is made from wheat flour and the filling is made from vegetables and meat. The "skin" is wrapped around the filling – this is a dumpling. The white "skin" wrapped around the filling makes them look both cute and pretty. In the past, if one wanted to eat a meal of dumplings, it wasn't that easy because one had to make the dumpling "skins" oneself, so if one person eats 20 dumplings, 10 people for a meal will need to make over 200 dumpling "skins". Furthermore, using vegetables and meat to make the stuffing will also take a long time. However, making dumplings is still a lot simpler than cooking dishes. Especially nowadays, living is very convenient (because ready-made) dumpling "skins" can be bought everywhere and so making dumplings to entertain people is even easier.

Because dumplings are easy to make, everyone likes to invite guests over for a meal of stuffed dumplings. Sometimes the host invites the guest to stuff the dumplings with him. Before stuffing the dumplings, everyone first washes their hands clean, then sits down together and, while stuffing the dumplings, talk and laugh. The host and guests together can chat about many many things. This way of entertaining guests is jolly and lively. Sometimes the children shout to be included, but in actual fact what they really want to do is play (at making) dumplings, not stuff dumplings. They form the dumpling into strange shapes and so the pure white dumplings are transformed into black ones in their hands – how can one eat a dumpling like that?

When all the dumplings have been stuffed, one can begin to cook them. How are they cooked? This is even easier. First boil the water and then place the dumplings into the water. After about 10 minutes when each dumpling has risen to the top, one can lift the dumplings out and eat them. Looking at the steaming dumplings makes everyone's mouth water.

Each white, shiny dumpling is very pretty, and sometimes you can see the filling inside the dumplings. You will often hear everyone joke around saying: "This beautiful dumpling must be the one that I wrapped!" If you see a strange-looking dumpling, you will hear other people joke: "This is the one you made!" Actually, no matter what they look like, they are all equally delicious when eaten.

Although making dumplings is an easy matter, however Chinese people are able to use different ways to make them. For example, use different meat or use different vegetables. When the filling is different, the flavor of the dumplings will also be different, and in this way, all sorts of different tastes appear.

Not only do the ingredients differ, the manner in which they are cooked is different as well. Boiling the dumplings is the most common method. Because they are cooked in water they are called "Water Dumplings". Dumplings can also be cooked without water but fried in oil instead. This is a different kind of dumpling and the flavor is quite special and very delicious. Some people prefer eating water dumplings, while others especially prefer eating dumplings fried in oil.

In days gone by, dumplings were only eaten during the New Year celebration. When stuffing the dumplings, some people will intentionally place a coin inside the dumpling. The belief was that the person who ate the dumpling with the coin in it would have a very good year this year. So if you have an opportunity to celebrate the New Year with a Chinese family and eat dumplings, you had best first ask if any coins were put into the stuffing made today. On no account eat too quickly or else you may incur stomach problems.

Nowadays people can eat dumplings at any time of the year. One can buy ready-made dumpling "skins" and dumpling filling in the market, and some businesses even sell stuffed dumplings. There are some people whose business is selling ready-made dumplings as well as some factories which can make lots of dumplings at once. So it has become more and more convenient to eat dumplings. When guests come to one's home, it only takes a few minutes to prepare steaming hot, tasty dumplings.

Although dumplings are very easy to make, actually they are very tasty and also represent the kind regards of the host. That is the most special thing about them. The Chinese love the merriment that comes when sitting and eating dumplings together, and chatting and joking together. If, one day, a Chinese person invites you to their home to eat dumplings, all you have to do is to accept!

Chapter 7   Three Generations under One Roof

A long time ago not many people were able to have the opportunity to go to school in China, so children from a young age learned everything by imitating their mothers and fathers. If Dad farmed fields, the children followed him around and learned how to farm. If Dad was a businessman, the children also followed him around and learned how to do business. By the time they had grown up, got married, and had children of their own, they would still live together with their mother and father and wouldn't leave their original home. This kind of grandparents, parents and children all living together in one household is called "Three Generations under One Roof".

A family of three generations under one roof is commonly seen in China. In the past, Chinese used to consider that the more people the better, so each family had many children. When the children had grown up and got married, everyone still lived together. The children's children continued having lots of babies, and in this way a family grew bigger and bigger, and the family members therefore became more and more in number. Sometimes a family was no longer three generations but four or five generations under the same roof. Everyone was of the opinion that the larger the family, the more they were blessed with good fortune and so didn't worry that others might come and give them trouble.

Emperors in former times also liked large families very much and considered that they had many advantages. In ancient times there was a family that had over 700 members so the emperor went to see them and even presented them with many gifts. The nation in those days hoped that every family would have many children, because the more the people, the more powerful the country would be, and so would not fear other countries coming and giving them trouble.

In "Three Generations under One Roof", the first generation are the grandparents. Their status in the family is the highest. All important decisions must obtain their agreement. They are the oldest and also comparatively more knowledgeable, so whenever anyone has a problem, they will go to ask them. The grandparents will also enjoy helping out and pass on any knowledge they have to the children.

In "Three Generations under One Roof", the parents are the second generation. Their work is the heaviest: on the one hand, they will look after the elderly grandparents, taking care of their health and making their lives happy; on the other hand, they also need to take care of the children and keep an eye on their homework. Being a parent (means) during the daytime working hard and in the evening also having lots to do in the home. Their health is usually the best in the family, but their job is also the hardest.

In "Three Generations under One Roof", the children represent the third generation. They have the nicest life of all. Normally their parents will look after them; if the parents are out working, the grandparents will take care of them. Grandparents love children best of all. Whatever the children want, the grandparents will give to them. If the children have done something wrong which has made their parents angry, the grandparents will step in and put in a good word for the children. Children truly are the happiest of all in the family!

What advantages are there in having three generations under one roof? In previous times many Chinese were farmers. The one thing farming most needs is help from family members, so with so many family members, they can all help together to get the work done. The grandparents can help with some of the simpler jobs; the harder work is done by the parents, and of course the children will also help their parents with some of the easier household chores. In this way, with the whole family doing it together, everything can be completed very quickly.

By the evening, after finishing the evening meal, when all the work has been done, the whole family goes out to sit in the courtyard. Everyone is together in the courtyard talking and relaxing. At this time the grandparents will tell stories to the children that they had heard before. These were stories that their grandparents' grandparents had also told them. The more the children listened, the more they enjoyed listening and wanted their grandparents to tell them stories every day!

The grandparents look after the children, the parents look after the grandparents, and the children bring joy to their grandparents, because each person needs the attention and care of others. Chinese people often tell their children that they must be filial to their parents. So, what is "filial piety"? It means obeying one's parents and not to cause them any sadness. In a family where there are three generations under one roof, children from when they are young observe how their parents show filial piety towards the grandparents. As time goes by, when they have grown up, they too will be filial to their parents. In this way, as one generation follows another, everyone has learned how to be filial.

The Chinese regard the family as very important. If a member of the family does something good, everyone will be very pleased – it seems as if the entire family had done something good. If a member of the family has done something wrong or done something bad, the whole family will feel as if they had all done the wrong or bad thing. Therefore each member is always very careful, not wishing to let everyone down.

Nowadays, Chinese families do not have lots of children like before. People in the past used to think that to have children was so that there would be someone to take care of them in their old age. (Although) that way of thinking has now slowly changed, however there are still many families living with three generations under one roof. And why (does this still exist)? Actually, being filial to one's parents and taking care of one's children is not necessarily done in the hope of obtaining some benefit – what is most important is the happiness that the whole family living together brings. "Family" in Chinese people's eyes will always be the most important.

Chapter 8   The Water Splashing Festival — a Folk Custom from the Southwest

China is a very large country. From ancient times right up to the present, there have been many different ethnic groups living there. In China, the ethnic group with the largest population is the Han people group, also known as the Han people. In the previous texts in this book, the social customs you read about are mainly those of the Han people group. Apart from the Han people group, the population of the other ethnic groups is comparatively less in number, so they are called minority people groups. And so do these minority people groups also have many special social customs? Let us read about them together!

In the southwestern part of China, there are many high mountains and large rivers. Because the mountains are high and the water is deep, it is very inconvenient going from one place to another, so people from one area had very little contact with people who live in another area. So as time went by, each area slowly developed its own culture and ways of living. In the end, the people from these areas became numerous small ethnic groups. The southwest region of China has the most minority groups (than any other region in China).

There is one minority people group in the southeast of China, and they have an unusual festival called the "Water Splashing Festival". Each time the Water Splashing Festival comes round, everybody splashes water on everyone else. Those who get splashed are not angry, on the contrary they are actually very happy about it.

How did this peculiar tradition come about? According to legend, it all started with an ancient story....

A long, long time ago in this area there lived a very scary man. He often came out and ate people, so all the people who lived in the area were very afraid of him. This person had seven beautiful wives who were also frightened of him and really disliked him. In order to help the local people live in peace, one evening, they killed their terrible husband.

Although the horrible man was dead, the strange thing was that his head was still alive. The seven wives took the head and threw it into the river. But as soon as the head was thrown into the river, the water in the river became very hot and all the fish in the river died from the heat. Then they threw the head onto the ground but nothing would grow on the ground anymore. Finally the seven of them had no choice but to take turns carrying his head – one person for one day. When the one who had been carrying the head had finished her turn, everyone hurriedly poured water on her to help clean off the filth. In the end, in order to express the people's gratitude to the seven women, the Water Splashing Festival became an annual event.

The Water Splashing Festival of this region resembles the Han people's New Year. At this time, there are all sorts of fun activities going on everywhere. On the first day of the festival, one doesn't splash water on each other, instead they have boat-rowing competitions on the large rivers. Everybody feels happy for those who come first. Some people sing and some dance. Then on the second day, the water splashing begins! No matter whether they are men or women, children or older people, everyone splashes water on everyone else. You splash me and I splash you. The more one gets splashed, the more fortunate one is because water helps get rid of bad things and so life in the coming year will be even better.

Therefore, if you ever go there and water is splashed all over you by someone, on no account get angry, but rather you should be pleased. You'd better throw some water on someone else too!

The evening of the Water Splashing Festival is even livelier. Everyone goes to the same place. The sound of singing and laughter is everywhere. Some people dance and others clap. Some people get so happy that they drink wine, sing and dance all at the same time, almost forgetting themselves! There are also very many people who come here to watch the Water Splashing Festival. And so in this way, it's not until very late at night that things finally quieten down here.

There is also another special activity which happens at the Water Splashing Festival. If one person falls in love with another person, he/she will give that person something he/she (i.e. the giver) likes. So if someone gives you something, you can be sure that the person has taken a liking for you. Also related to this activity, someone may take the opportunity when others are not looking to take away some personal belonging. This is also because they have taken a fancy for the other person. If you have an opportunity to participate in the Water Splashing Festival and you discover that one of your possessions is missing, maybe someone has fallen in love with you!

There are many other minority people groups in the southwest of China and they also have many special festivals. There is one minority people group that lives high up in the mountains where it is very cold. There it is very inconvenient to bathe and so they seldom take a bath. However, they have a "Bathing Festival". The Bathing Festival takes place when the weather is warm and the water in the river is not so cold, and so everybody goes into the river to bathe together. Because there are so many people, the originally clean river water turns dark all of a sudden. There aren't many opportunities in the year when one can take a bath, so as soon as the Bathing Festival arrives, everyone is terrifically happy!

Also there are some minority people groups who have singing competitions or horse racing competitions on their festivals. All the southwestern minority groups love singing and horse-riding, and the best of all is when everyone is happily together. They also have their own ethnic group's New Year which takes place on a different date from the Han people's New Year. At New Year, everyone will drink a little wine and will eat some of their group's local specialties.

China is a vast land, the population is large, and there are many ethnic groups. From the past right up until the present, the different ethnic groups each have their own different culture. Their festivals are different, and so are their activities. However there is one point which is the same – it is that everyone wants to live peaceably and happily. In the end, the differences between some minorities have become less distinct and they have become one family.

Chapter 9 Education in Ancient Times

In China over 2500 years ago there was a famous man whose name was Confucius. He came up with some very important ideas. He considered that, no matter whether or not a person had money or status, everyone ought to go and get an education, learning the proper principles of "being" and "doing". The teaching method was to teach each child according to his or her own unique characteristics. Confucius' idea was extremely good and everyone considers him to be ancient China's first great teacher. His ideas formed the beginnings of Chinese educational thinking, and right up to the present time, these (educational) ideas still ring true and remain useful.

The most important aspect of educating children, according to the Chinese, is the desire that children know how to conduct themselves appropriately. A well-mannered person should know when to stand and when to sit. No matter what the situation, one must be polite. Everyone believes that a person can take care of his own and his family's affairs only if he is well educated; only a person who takes good care of his and his family's affairs can then take care of the country's affairs; only a person who takes good care of his own country's affairs can bring peace in this world. Therefore, when educating a person, one must start with the small things and only then can one move onto the larger matters.

In ancient times some people learned in school and others learned at home. Also the schools in ancient times were different from schools today. Public schools were very few in number, and most schools were run by the teacher himself. The schools were comparatively small and there weren't many students either. Those who came to study were all of different ages. Some pupils started when they were young, others only came to study after they had grown up.

All the pupils were boys, and at that time only very few girls were allowed to study. A beautiful, ancient Chinese love story tells about a girl who really wanted to go to school to study, but all the pupils who went to study at that time were boys. So she dressed in boy's clothing and made herself look just like a boy. Consequently, in the school she got to know one of her classmates, a boy who at first had no idea that she was a girl. The two studied and played together. In the end, the story about the two of them became a love story.

In ancient times, education meant reading books written by historical people. The books had poems in them, as well as much on the principles of personal conduct and how to handle one's affairs (i.e. how to "be" and to "do"). Besides studying from books, in school the teacher used other methods to educate the children, for instance playing the zither, playing chess, writing characters, painting pictures, etc., because everyone believed that this kind of education could help a person become a truly useful human being.

According to the Chinese, playing the zither is a great way to educate someone. When learning to play the zither, only by putting everything into playing it will one produce beautiful music. Listening to the beautiful sound of the zither will put people into a good state of mind. In addition, a person can use the sounds the zither makes to express their feelings, and with the sound of this instrument he can teach himself and others to attain some of the principles of good conduct.

Playing chess is another method of educating someone. The Chinese normally like to play "Go". So, what help can children get from playing "Go"? It can help children, when encountering difficulties, to not be nervous or anxious, (but rather) to be able to contemplate quietly. Playing "Go" can also help children to look at a problem very clearly when a change occurs. It also can help them attain the confidence and ability to deal with problems.

Calligraphy is another method of educating children. Chinese often say: (literally) characters as that person. The meaning of this phrase is that by looking at a person's handwriting, you can almost tell what kind of a person they are. But, for people writing characters in ancient times, it was not as convenient as it is nowadays. In those days everyone used a writing brush to write with. If, when writing, you pressed down (on the brush) too hard, the characters would be both dark and ugly. If you didn't use enough force, the characters would be both slender and not pleasing to the eye. Therefore, when writing characters with a brush, the pressure of the hand has to be just right to be okay. When writing characters, one definitely also needs to concentrate as well as practice often. So, many famous historical figures would practice for a long while each day.

Painting is also a good opportunity for learning. But have you discovered that Chinese paintings in ancient times were quite special? That kind of style is called Chinese painting or traditional Chinese painting. Objects in a traditional painting don't look quite like the real objects themselves, because the important thing in Chinese painting is not to paint what the eye can see – mountains, water, flowers, grass and trees – what they really look like, but rather what the heart feels they are like, so painting is a good method of education. It allows children many opportunities to use their imagination, to understand and to love the brighter side of life, and at the same time to produce a greater interest in studying. So those children who like painting, their minds will become even more attentive and beautiful.

Whether it be playing the zither, playing chess, practicing calligraphy, or painting pictures, they all contribute to a child's healthy growth and help that child obtain a real education. They can teach a child to master how not to be saddened by trifling matters, and also how not to lose confidence in the face of insignificant difficulties. When they encounter a problem, they can quietly think of a solution. When there is a lot to do, they know how to accomplish them one at a time.

Every little detail in life can be used to educate children. However, in ancient times only very few people were able to study. Some, from when they were young, had to help their parents do things, and so had no time or money to study, and were (therefore) illiterate. In spite of this, Chinese parents would still tell their children the principles of appropriate personal behavior. Home was their school, their parents were their teachers, and the matters of daily life became the subjects they studied. So, some people went to school to study, others learned at home, but everyone hoped that their own children became useful members (of society).

Chapter 10   The Dragon Boat Festival — Dragon Boats and Zongzi

Probably about 2300 years ago, China was divided into seven small countries. These seven small countries constantly attacked each other, none of them ever giving way to the other. Among them was a small country in the south of China called Chu. In the country of Chu lived a very patriotic man whose name was Qu Yuan. Qu Yuan helped the king and country in many ways. He often discovered problems in the country and so told the king how to resolve them. He was a very talented man and everyone liked him.

The king also liked Qu Yuan because he helped him so much. There were, however, a few people who didn't like Qu Yuan. They were very unhappy to see how much the king liked Qu Yuan, so they began to say bad things about Qu Yuan in front of the king. When the king heard these things, he thought they were true and (so) was very angry; the king slowly changed his mind about Qu Yuan and started to dislike him.

The king had a bad habit – he most enjoyed hearing other people say nice things about him. If someone flattered the king, he would like him very much. There were some bad people who knew about the king's (bad) habit so they constantly flattered him. The more the king listened, the happier he was, and began to spend lots of time with these evil men, so the king more and more didn't enjoy listening to what Qu Yuan said. One day, the king was very unhappy about something Qu Yuan had said. He was so angry that he banished Qu Yuan to a place very far away. In an instant, Qu Yuan's life had changed completely.

Qu Yuan stayed indoors every day and his heart was very sad. When he was sad he wrote poems, and when he had written the poems, he felt even sadder. He wrote very many poems. In them he wrote about his feelings, his love for his country, and what he wanted to say to the king. But the king knew absolutely nothing about Qu Yuan's (personal) matters after he had left (the king's court). In the end, Qu Yuan became more and more miserable and felt that life was no longer worth living. He came to a riverbank, looked at the water, thought about the state of the nation, and then plunged into the river. He hoped that, in this way, the king would understand how he felt. He also hoped that, by his death, he could tell the king that he should govern his country well and never again listen to the flattery of evil men.

All those who were acquainted with Qu Yuan knew that he was very patriotic, so when they heard that he had jumped into the river, they all rushed to the riverbank to look for him. Several people went up and down the river in small wooden boats looking for him, and others shouted out his name from the riverbank. But no one ever found him. People feared that his body had been eaten by a fish so they thought up an idea: they used leaves and wrapped rice up in them, then dropped them into the river. This kind of rice wrapped in leaves later became the "Zongzi" which Chinese eat. People hoped that the fish would come and eat the rice instead of his body.

Because the day Qu Yuan died happened to be the 5th day of the 5th month of the Chinese lunar calendar, so after then, every year on the 5th day of the 5th month, people remember Qu Yuan – the patriotic poet. Everyone had hoped that Qu Yuan hadn't in fact died and that they would find him one day, so on this day, many people still would go out in boats and put zongzi in the river. As time went by, more and more people knew about this, so each year at this time, in many areas of China lots of people commemorate Qu Yuan. So in the end, this day became one of China's very important holidays, called Dragon Boat Festival.

The Dragon Boat Festival is one of the three most important festivals in China and each year falls on the 5th day of the 5th month of the Chinese lunar calendar. Because it is the 5th day of the 5th month, so a long while ago people called this day Dragon Boat Festival. In the end, people knew that Qu Yuan was not alive anymore, and so no longer threw zongzi into the river at this time each year. However, at Dragon Boat Festival, every family will make lots of zongzi to eat. Everyone wraps the zongzi, eats them, and while telling their children the story of the poet who loved his country, remembers Qu Yuan with affection.

The Dragon Boat Festival occurs during the time just when the farmers are not very busy and can take time to rest. At this time, people no longer go out looking for Qu Yuan in boats, but everyone still enjoys remembering this patriotic poet by rowing boats. So in many places in China there are boat races on the 5th day of the 5th month each year. Chinese really like dragons because they believe that they are a dragon's descendants. People later on made their boats into a special shape – the bow of the boat looks like a dragon's head; the outside of the boat is painted in many pretty colors. They call this type of boat a "Dragon Boat". Over 10 people can sit in one of these boats. Each year during the Dragon Boat Festival, all the big rivers have many dragon boat races. As soon as the race starts, everyone rows very hard because everyone wants to come first.

Today the Dragon Boat Festival is already an important Chinese holiday. Chinese people will all think of eating zongzi on this day. Although ready-made zongzi are available everywhere, many households, especially farming families, still prefer to make their own to eat. If a person works away from home and can't get back, his parents will ask someone to take him some zongzi to eat. Some people are by themselves or aren't married, or their home is far away, so their friend will invite them to eat zongzi. Or else he will go outside and buy some to eat. So if you don't eat any zongzi at Dragon Boat Festival, everyone will feel it is very strange, as though one had forgotten to do something important.

In ancient times, if there was a boat race, everyone would rush to see the excitement, and furthermore there would be people selling things and others buying things on the riverbank. When the race began, the riverbank became even livelier – the sound of people, the splashing of the water, sounds of laughter and shouting could all be heard at the same time. It was truly interesting! Nowadays the dragon boat races are still an important part of Dragon Boat Festival in many regions.

When Dragon Boat Festival takes place it is normally when it is hottest. At this time, the farmers can rest at home for a while, preparing for the busy work that will follow straight on (after the festival). With the hot weather, people easily get tired and have no strength to work in the fields, so farmers usually drink a little wine at this time; it is said that drinking alcohol can prevent sickness and help people bear the heat. This should not be an excuse for drinking alcohol!

The Dragon Boat Festival is one of the big Chinese festivals of the year. This holiday causes people to remember the patriotic poet Qu Yuan, and his story lets people understand why Chinese go out on dragon boats and eat zongzi each year.

Chapter 11   Old Customs — The Lying-In Period after Childbirth and Foot Binding

For a long time now, Chinese culture has had many special customs. Some of these cultural customs are good, others are not. Some of them today we can comprehend, others we cannot. Some of them people cannot accept today. But no matter what, there are many Chinese customs everyone has still followed since childhood. So what special customs still exist amongst Chinese people today?

For example, matters concerning giving birth to a child. In ancient times, before the child was born, the mother had to pay attention to many things. If someone was pregnant, she couldn't pick up anything in the house just as she likes, because in those days people believed that if a mother wasn't careful and picked up just whatever household thing she wanted, her child might be born disfigured: it might have an extra eye or be missing a hand. Even right up until today, if someone gives birth to an odd-looking child, other people will still believe that it was definitely because the mother wasn't careful about the things she picked up.

There is one very old custom that possibly still influences every Chinese family today – this is the "lying-in period after childbirth". And what is the "lying-in period after childbirth"? It is the period after childbirth when the mother must spend one month at home until she is allowed to go out. This is because the mother had a hard time for 10 months before giving birth. After the birth the mother's health is not at all good so she needs to rest at home for one month. Some people will ask: "Isn't this a really good thing?" However, having to stay in one's home for a whole month (without going out) is not what the mother really enjoys!

During this month, the mother must eat a lot of (nutritious) food in order to restore her health back to normal. Much of this food is cooked together with Chinese herbal medicine: fish cooked with Chinese herbal medicine, chicken cooked with Chinese herbal medicine, and pork cooked with Chinese herbal medicine. Just as soon as the mother has finished eating one fish, her family is (already) cooking another one for her to eat. Just as soon as she has finished eating a chicken, another cooked one is placed in front of her. Even delicious food will become unsavory if eaten too much. Even though young mothers don't like it, they must still keep on eating it, because elderly people will say that this lying-in period after birth is beneficial for one's health. Only when the lying-in period is done properly will the mother's health be restored to normal, and the next time when she gives birth, only then will that child grow to be healthy.

There are also many (other) things to pay attention to during the lying-in period after childbirth. The mother may not eat any cold food, may not pick up any heavy object, may not sit in a draft, and may not wash her hair. Every day her old grandmother will tell her not to do this and not to do that; you must eat this and you must eat that. Think about it – one (whole) month without washing your hair – what a horrible thought, so many mothers feel that spending one (whole) month at home is too long!

There were also many (other) special cultural customs in ancient times. Foot binding was one of the most bizarre of them. Foot binding was wrapping girls' feet very tightly with cloth bandages in order to prevent them from growing. Why was this done? There is a legend about it. A long long while ago, there was an emperor who really liked a (young) woman. This young woman was very petite and was very good at dancing. One day she wrapped her feet in cloth to make them (appear) small. When she started dancing, she looked especially beautiful and the emperor was ecstatic when he saw her and so he demanded that all the women in the whole country bind their feet. The emperor said: the smaller the feet, the more beautiful the woman.

From this time onwards, foot binding became a tradition. In order for the feet to become small, 4–5 year-old girls must bind up their feet and only once every few days were they allowed to unwrap them and wash them. When the feet were clean, they must be wrapped up again. The most difficult part was to wrap them so as to maintain them at their original small size. But as the girls grew, so did their feet. Their feet hurt a lot when they were bound small. Often, because of the pain, they couldn't stand up properly or sit still. Some girls cried to their parents not to bind their feet again, but their mother and father would cry and say to them: "Child! If you don't bind your feet now, no one will like you later, and no one will dare to take you in marriage."

In this way, as one year followed the next, the girls' feet remained tightly bound, so when they were fully grown women, their feet were truly very small – only 7–8 c.m. long. Because their feet were so terribly small, they were unable to stand for very long or walk any distance. When walking they usually needed someone to help them. Their gait resembled a flower being blown back and forth in the breeze. At that time, people considered women with bound feet to be the most beautiful, so all Chinese women in former times followed the custom of binding one's feet.

Nowadays people know much more. People know that not only foot binding is very bad for the body, but also that it is an unacceptable cultural custom. Women should not have to have their feet bound, and women with small feet are not necessarily beautiful, so slowly young women never again bound their feet. In some places today one can still see some old ladies with bound feet; however this ancient cultural custom is no longer seen on young women's feet.

Many people have discovered that a lot of the Chinese social cultural customs are related to women; this is because Chinese culture attaches comparatively greater importance to men, so men are allowed to do many of the things they like, but there are many things a women can't do. In this day and age things are not the same. The changes in Chinese society are enormous, so although men and women are still not very equal, modern Chinese women are a lot better off than those before.

Chapter 12 Mid-Autumn Festival — Moon Viewing and Moon Cakes

What a large round moon! This is the most beautiful of views at Mid-Autumn Festival. Each year on the 15th day of the 8th month of the Chinese lunar calendar is the Mid-Autumn Festival. Many people know that the Chinese lunar calendar is calculated according to the changes in the moon. The 15th day of each month is a full moon, so each year when the 15th day of the 8th month comes round, everyone will sense that the moon looks especially round and big. On this evening, every household will prepare lots of delicious moon cakes and fruit. The whole family sits outside enjoying the moon and chatting together. The children are busy playing with their own things.

In addition to the Spring Festival and Dragon Boat Festival which were introduced earlier, the Mid-Autumn Festival is also an extremely important festival. On this day, many people who work away from home return to be with their family. This is because the Chinese have a saying "In the sky the moon is round; on earth the family is complete". Each member of the family is very important, and if one person is absent, the family is not complete.

Everyone considers that the day of the Mid-Autumn Festival is the moon's birthday. There are some ancient stories related to this line of reasoning. According to one story, a long long while ago there once was a goddess whose husband was very strong. At that time, 10 suns appeared in the sky and the weather was extremely hot. Many trees, animals, and human beings died from the heat. There was no water to drink and the people almost couldn't continue living on (under these circumstances). At this moment, the goddess' husband arrived. He knocked nine of the suns out of the sky, leaving only one. From then on, the weather changed being neither (too) cold nor (too) hot. The people's life began to get better once again. Everyone was very grateful to him, so they decided to let him be king.

However, the goddess' husband became ever more evil after he was made king. He spent all his time in merriment and didn't care about the affairs of his people, and when he was in a bad mood, he simply killed people. He also felt that the people ought to be forever thankful to him. Thereupon people's life once again became as bitter as before. One day the king got hold of a kind of magic potion. It was said that those who took the potion would never ever die. When the people knew about this, they were terrified, because if the king kept on living, their days would for ever be miserable.

At this time, the goddess knew what the people were thinking. One day, when the king wasn't at home, she took the opportunity to take out the potion. It just so happened that just then the king came home and, as soon as the goddess got nervous, she swallowed the potion. When she had swallowed it, her body became very light and at once started flying upwards. She flew higher and higher towards the sky. When the king saw this, he was very angry and shouted to her: "Come back! Come back!"

The gods in the heavens didn't like this goddess who had suddenly flown in, because they felt that she shouldn't take other people's things just as she liked. The goddess knew that she couldn't live in the heavens with the rest of the gods, so she felt that the best thing to do was to go and fly to the moon and live there. For several thousand years now, Chinese have always believed that there really is a goddess living on the moon. Every year when the Mid-Autumn Festival comes round, everyone will worship the moon and thank the goddess for rescuing them.

The goddess actually doesn't live by herself on the moon. Legend has it that there is also a little white rabbit with her. If you look at the moon very carefully, you'll discover a small dark thing on it. Chinese are of the opinion that those are the eyes of the little white rabbit. The little white rabbit works hard at night and only gets to rest during the daytime. The ancients tell us that our good life today is brought about by this rabbit's hard work at night.

During the Mid-Autumn Festival, everyone eats a type of thing called "Moon Cake". Moon cakes are round, and there are large ones and small ones. The cakes are filled with all kinds of filling and are extremely delicious. Each time this day arrives, everyone will buy moon cakes to give as gifts to relatives and friends. Those who sell moon cakes are the happiest because business is so good at this time every year. Some people who receive moon cakes are worried that they won't be able to eat them all so they give them to somebody else. In this way, you give me moon cakes and I give you moon cakes, and sometimes people receive moon cakes which they had given to somebody else a few days earlier!

At spring each year, from morning until evening, farmers are hard at it planting their fields each day, (so there is) no (time to) rest. Everyone hopes that what has been planted may grow quickly, (and so) in autumn there will be a good harvest. When autumn arrives and everyone sees that what they planted has grown in abundance, their hearts are truly happy because they needn't worry about having nothing to eat in winter. So, when the Mid-Autumn Festival comes round, everyone is in a happy mood. When they look at the moon, they feel it is even more big and round.

On the evening of the Mid-Autumn Festival, the entire family sits in the courtyard chatting and telling stories. The evening breeze blows gently and the stars in the sky are beautiful. At this time, when everyone is eating moon cakes and looking at the moon, it is truly one of life's happiest moments.

Chapter 13   Birthday Banquet and the Newborn's Name

Even though everybody must die some day, Chinese still hope for a long and good life. And so because of this, you will be able to do many things that you set out to do and life will be even happier. From ancient times right up until today, people have hoped to be able to discover the secret of long life.

It is said that, in the past, there is a potion in China which, when taken, people won't die, nor will you ever get old or sick, so everybody would like to get hold of this potion. But does it really exist somewhere on this earth? Nobody knows and nobody has ever seen it. However, in China there is another method which it has been said can make people live a little longer: this method is the Birthday Banquet.

On the day of the birthday, the most important person is the one celebrating his or her birthday, so everybody hopes that him or her have a happy birthday. The family members will cook a lot of delicious food, and sometimes will invite a few good friends to eat it together (with them). Previously, if the celebration was for a boy, the family will buy lots of gifts for him as presents as well as the family inviting guests (for the meal). However, if the celebration was for a girl, everyone felt that it wasn't so important.

The birthday celebrations include a special kind of noodle. This kind of noodle is both thin and long. It is said that those who eat it will live a long life. Chinese call this type of noodle "Long Life Noodle". Having a long life is regarded as important and blessed in

China. If the person celebrating his/her birthday is already elderly, those who have gone to eat the birthday banquet (with him/her) will express their congratulations by saying, for example: "Wish you longevity as the south mountain, blessing as the east sea". Old people feel very happy when they hear (these words), and will thank everyone for coming and celebrating their birthday with them.

Chinese people hope to live a long and good life. Old people will celebrate old age, and children must be given a good name as soon as they are born. Chinese believe that if the name is good, then their entire life will be good. China is a society centered on the family. As soon as the child is born, it will be given the same surname as the father's. However, the child's name must be thought about very carefully. Before the child is born, the parents and grandparents are already thinking about the child's name.

If it is a boy, everyone wants him to have good fortune, so the character "福" (blessing, happiness) is often used in boy's names. If it is a girl, everyone hopes that she will grow to be very pretty, so the character "美" (pretty, beautiful) is often used in girl's names. The hope is that they will resemble the beauty of their names. However, in ancient times, if a child was born with a physical problem, the family would intentionally give the child a bad-sounding name, because it was said that the uglier the name was, the easier it was to raise the child. It would be like a nameless weed which no one pays any attention to but which still manages to live very well.

Because Chinese regard males more highly than females, so everyone hopes to give birth to a boy. If they gave birth to a girl, their name would often have the meaning of "younger brother come quickly" in it, for example "beckon younger brother" or "connect to a boy". The meaning is that they hope the mother would give birth to a boy next time. In the past, girls had almost no social status in China because everyone felt that giving birth to a girl was of no use at all to the home, furthermore when the girl had grown up, she would be married off to someone else and so would become the member of someone else's family.

Chinese people are of the opinion that if you want to live a good life, one must have a good name. So, after the family had decided on a name for the child, the name had to be verified by a scholarly person. If, in the past, there had been a person with the same name who had lived a good life, then the name is a good one. If, in the past, there had been a person with the same name who had lived an unfortunate life, then the name isn't a good one. So finding a good name for a newborn child is not an easy task.

The birthday banquet is eaten in the hope of living a long life, and the newborn is given a good name in the hope of having a happy life. The Chinese doing things this way seems a little funny. However, in China, doing it in this way will actually be quite helpful, because when eating the birthday banquet, it can make everyone happy who celebrates their birthdays; listening to kind words can make the mind focus on good things, and living will have new hope. Eating a little more good food can make a person healthier. If a person's mood is good and his/her health is good too, won't he/she then be able to live a little longer?

Everybody wishes to have a good name, and likes people with good names, because when family and friends call his name, he will be reminded of the meaning of his name. He will slowly fix in his mind the meaning of his name and often recall what his parents' hopes had been for his life. In this way, a good name can really help a person lead a conscientious and hard-working life, and will be able to live a good life. Often some of these peculiar Chinese cultural customs do have truth in them; however, these cultural customs all still take the man to be the most important; this is because men have always been more important in China. Men have always got more than women, and so obviously society expects more from them.

Chapter 14 The Double Ninth Festival

When the Mid-Autumn Festival is over, the weather begins to get cooler. The 7th, 8th and 9th month of the Chinese lunar calendar are the autumn months. When the 9th month arrives, it is almost the end of autumn. At this time the weather will change and it gets cooler and then cold. Sometimes it will even snow! Every year at this time, if the weather is nice and people have time, they will go outside to enjoy themselves, because later on the weather will get colder and colder, so one won't be able to go out anymore. There is a festival during the 9th month of the Chinese lunar calendar called "Double Ninth Festival".

"Double Ninth Festival" each year falls on the 9th day of the 9th month (of the lunar calendar). The Chinese like the number "9" very much because the word "jiu" (nine) and the word "jiu" (long) are pronounced the same. "99" sounds just like "everlasting", which signifies everlasting peace. In China, a person who can live for a long time is considered a fortunate person, so for this reason the 9th day of the 9th month is "Old People's Day" in China. Everyone hopes that their own parents and their elderly relatives can live to an old age – until 99 years old. On this day everyone will give the elderly some very nice things in the hope that they will live even longer and that their life will be an even happier one.

In the past, on the day of the Double Ninth Festival, people used to take some delicious food, change into comfortable clothes and then go to a more elevated area (i.e. climb hills), because they believed that, by being higher up, they would be closer to the gods up in the sky and the gods would be able to hear what they were saying.

But in regard to the Double Ninth Festival, there is also this ancient legend. One year, on the day after the Mid-Autumn Festival, a god in the heavens spoke to a young person and said: "Something big is going to happen in the vicinity of your home: on the 9th day of the 9th month all the people and animals in that area will die, unless on that day you rush to the mountains and also drink some chrysanthemum wine – only if you do this will death and other terrible things not befall you."

When the young man heard this, he ran home to tell his family and his relatives and friends nearby. Thereupon, on the 9th day of the 9th month they all left their homes and climbed up a mountain. In the end, when they returned home, they saw that all the people and animals that hadn't left their homes were already dead. From then on, on the 9th day of the 9th month, people will go up to the mountains, and so this day became one of China's cultural festivals.

Nowadays on the Double Ninth Festival each year, many families will take their children to go and climb mountains. It has already become a significant family activity. When climbing the mountain, everyone stops and then goes, goes and then stops. When they are tired from walking, they all stop and take a rest. While resting, they can sit by the side of the road, eat some snacks and drink some water. When they have rested enough, they continue to climb upwards.

The weather in autumn is the most pleasant. Although everyone feels a little tired when they climb, they also feel very happy. The air is great on the top, and everybody feels great too. In this way, everyone walks all the way to the highest point.

When one arrives at the top and takes a look, there are already a lot of other people up there. On the mountain-top there are chrysanthemums everywhere. There are yellow ones and white ones – all the different colors of the chrysanthemums together look extremely beautiful. The chrysanthemum doesn't mind cold weather. Even though the weather gets colder and colder, the chrysanthemum keeps on blooming beautifully. So, from the past right up until the present, the Chinese have always been fond of the chrysanthemum. Furthermore, when painting, people also like to paint it.

At Double Ninth Festival there are "Chrysanthemum Fairs" in many places. At this time, all the different chrysanthemums are placed next to each other – looking just like an ocean of chrysanthemums. Some people write poems about them, others paint them. Some people are busy selling chrysanthemums, others are busy buying them. There are also many people enjoying the flowers with rapt attention. Children are running all around, and all sorts of voices can be heard, sometimes loud sometimes soft; there are people everywhere, and the area is bustling with activity.

The flowers of the chrysanthemum are not only nice looking, they also can be taken and eaten. During the Double Ninth Festival, everybody drinks chrysanthemum tea or chrysanthemum wine. Chinese people consider the chrysanthemum to be a kind of medicine. It is said that drinking chrysanthemum tea or chrysanthemum wine is very beneficial to one's health. They are also good for one's eyes. The chrysanthemum is good for so many things, so that is why the Chinese are so fond of it.

Looking down from the top of the mountain, one can see a long way. The houses down below have become very small. At this time, everyone feels just how small they are in this world. In the past, there was a very famous poet who looked down from a high peak during the Double Ninth Festival and wrote down a poem about longing for his family. In the end, each year everyone recalls his poem on Double Ninth Festival, and in the same way, in one's heart one will remember family and friends.

Nowadays, there is no chrysanthemum fair anymore during the Double Ninth Festival, and not as many people as before go up into the mountains. However, on the day of the festival, everyone will still think about their family members and the old people. After finishing work, some people will rush home to see their elderly parents. Some people, even though they aren't able to return home, will telephone or write a letter home asking how their parents have been recently. From time immemorial, the Chinese have never changed their minds about being filial towards their parents.

Chapter 15   The Story of Chinese Characters

A long long while ago, people were first able to talk and only later able to write. Before the written language was invented, after people had finished talking, they quickly forgot what they had (just) said. So people often forgot to do things, and some people did things and forgot what it was that they had done. Thereupon, the ancients wanted to find ways to record what had been said and done.

At first some people thought of using the method of tying a knot in a piece of string to remember things. When something happened, they tied one knot, when two things happened they tied two knots. Gradually, as more and more things happened, more and more knots were tied, and in the end everyone still forgot what the matters were. Later on, some people drew pictures in order to remember things: some drew on the ground, (but) after a few days it would rain and the picture disappeared; some painted on trees, but trees are round and it is difficult to paint on them; also, one can't take the tree away, so it's really inconvenient!

The ancient people thought about it from every angle. (Then) they saw that there were many bones on the ground by the side of their houses – these were bones left over from the meat that they had eaten. They looked and looked until they found some bones with a flatter surface and carved a picture on the bone. The result was that they discovered this method was pretty good, and so in this way, Chinese characters began to appear. Several thousand years later, people have found many bones like this under the ground. The bones had strange pictures carved onto them; these were characters drawn by ancient men and Chinese call them "Oracle Bone Writings".

How did people in ancient times use drawings to remember things? For example, in those days, when someone looked at the sun, he drew a "⊙". He said that the sun is round and the middle is a little dark. Everybody felt that what he said was correct. Later on, when someone saw that drawing, they knew that it signified "sun". From then on, the ancients used drawings in order to record many things, and they also used drawings to express their meanings to other people and to those who came after them.

Take a look – the character "月" actually looks a little like the moon up in the sky! Also the character "木" looks very much like a tree. There are many Chinese characters that actually look like the real thing. However, some people felt that drawing pictures was too troublesome, so they changed the drawings into simpler signs or symbols. In the end, people also felt that, although Chinese characters were good and convenient, there were still many ideas that they had no way to write down. Thereupon, Chinese people once again started to think of a way and used the original characters to invent new ones. For example, the character "明" means "very bright". What is the brightest thing in the world? Obviously it is the sun and the moon, (so if you) put a "日" together with a "月", it will be very bright. This is how the character "明" came into being. From ancient times until now, through a very long period of transformation, these characters developed into the "Chinese characters" we are familiar with today.

A Chinese character can sometimes represent an idea. For example, "天" and "地". However, sometimes one needs two characters to represent an idea, such as "大家" or "东西". If you separated the two characters, it doesn't have the original meaning anymore. There are also 3-character and 4-character combinations that represent an idea, for example, "说一不二" which means that one should stand by what one says and not change (one's mind) or else others won't trust you anymore. This kind of four-character combination is called a "Four-Character Saying" by Chinese people. By simply using four characters, "Four-Character Sayings" can help people express complicated ideas simply and clearly.

There are also many Chinese characters with the same tone, for example "是", "事" and "市" are all pronounced the same, so in Chinese there are many ways of expressing things which are related to the pronunciation of the character. For example, if you go to a Chinese person's home, when giving a gift, you must remember never to give a clock. Why can't one give a clock as a gift? Because the words "送钟" (to give a clock) and "送终" (to give somebody a funeral) are pronounced (exactly) the same. If you give someone a clock, they may think that you hope they will die soon, and they will be very unhappy.

From ancient times right up until the present, the usage of Chinese characters is continually changing. If you get hold of something written by the ancients and look at it, many people are now unable to read it. What people wrote in ancient times is called classical Chinese. The writing and the spoken language nowadays are completely different from then. For this reason, modern people generally don't understand classical Chinese. Perhaps in several hundred years from now, people will not be able to understand our current written language.

Besides being used for remembering things, Chinese people often use Chinese characters in paintings. In earlier times, there were many famous people whose written characters were so beautiful that they looked like paintings. Some scholars also made writing characters their life's work. If their writing was beautifully done, there would be people who bought it and put it in their homes to enjoy. Apart from looking at the meaning of the characters, one also needs to look at the style of them. If Chinese characters are written well, they are as beautiful as a painting. Chinese call this kind of art "Calligraphy".

After reading these stories about Chinese characters, do you still feel that they are difficult (to learn)? By looking at the history of Chinese characters, people can know about a lot of interesting things. Isn't there a saying in English: "Practice makes perfect"? Learning how to write Chinese characters is the same truth. Chinese has a four-character saying: "Ability comes from long experience", so if you keep practicing, your Chinese characters will get better and better.

CHINESE MADE EASIER

实用速成汉语

CHINESE

CHARACTERS

6 - 60

The following characters have appeared in Lessons 6-60

— B —

ba	吧	(sentence suffix indicating suggestion or probability)
bā	八	8
bà	爸	dad
bái	白	white, bright; clear, pure; futile (effort)
bǎi	百	hundred
bài	拜	to worship
bān	班	a class (in school); (Measure for scheduled transport)
bān	搬	to move (something), to transport (goods)
bàn	半	half (a)
bàn	办	to manage/handle (a matter)
bāng	帮	to help, assist
bāo	包	to wrap (up); a parcel or package
bào	报	newspaper; to report; to recompense
bēi	杯	cup, glass, mug
běi	北	north
bèi	被	by (indicates the Passive); bed quilt
bèi	备	to prepare, be ready for
běn	本	volume (of books); (Measure for books)
bǐ	比	to compare; compared with; to compete
bǐ	笔	pen (general term for writing instruments)
bì	必	must, have to, necessarily, most certainly
biān	边	side
biàn	便	convenient, handy
biāo	表	a blank form, chart, meter; to show; relatives

bié	别	other; different; do not (imperative)
bǐng	饼	cookie, biscuit
bìng	病	illness, sickness, disease, to be sick; blemish, defect
bǔ	补	supplementary; nutritious; to mend, patch up
bù	不	not (the negative)
bù	步	a pace or step; to walk; on foot
bù	部	part, section; department; cabinet ministry

— C —

cái	才	only, just; just now; not until; natural talent
cài	菜	vegetable; dish (of food)
cān	餐	a meal; food
chā / chà	差	difference; mistake / nearly, approx.; differ, fall short
chá	茶	tea
chá	察	to investigate, examine, survey, scrutinize
chāi	差	to dispatch (someone on a mission or errand)
cháng	长	long
cháng	常	often, frequently; usually; common, ordinary
chǎng	场	arena/ground; act/performance (of a play or movie)
chāo	超	to exceed, be more than, surpass; to overtake
chǎo	炒	to stir-fry, to roast
chē	车	vehicle (general word)
chén	陈	(a Chinese family name)
chī	吃	to eat
chóng	重	to repeat, to do again
chū	出	out, exit; to (re)produce; to happen, occur
chú	除	except, besides; to get rid of; (in math) to divide

chǔ	楚	clear, distinct; neat; distress, suffering
chuān	穿	to wear or put on (clothes/shoes)
chuāng	窗	window
chūn	春	Spring (season)
cì	次	times; occasion; next in order; inferior, lower
cóng	从	from (a place or time)
cuò	错	wrong, incorrect

— D —

dǎ	打	to make (a phone call); hit, beat, fight; to do; to get
dà	大	big, large
dài	带	to take (along), to bring (along); to lead; a belt, tie
dān	单	a slip of paper; a list; odd (numbers); single, only
dàn	但	but, however; only, merely
dāng / dàng	当	ought to, should; the very same / to regard as
dào	道	Taoism; a way/principle; road, path
dào	到	to (a place/time); to arrive at
de	的	(Noun/Verb suffix of possession or modification)
dé / de	得	to get, to obtain / (a grammar particle)
dé	德	German; morals, virtues
děi	得	must, ought to
děng	等	to wait (for); when, until; etc., and so on
dì	地	place, location; ground, earth
dì	弟	younger brother
dì	第	(ordinalizing prefix to numbers)
diǎn	点	o'clock; (Measure for hours of the clock); point
diàn	店	shop, store, commercial establishment

diàn	电	electricity
dìng	定	definite, fixed; certainly; to decide or fix
dōng	东	east
dǒng	懂	to understand
dòng	动	to move
dōu	都	all, both; always
dòu	豆	beans, peas
dù	度	degree; (number of) times; to pass (through)
duǎn	短	short
duì	对	to be correct, right; to(wards)
duō	多	much, many; more

— E —

ér	儿	son
ér	而	but, and yet, nevertheless; also, and
èr	二	2

— F —

fā / fà	发	to start; to emit, give out / hair (on the head)
fǎ	法	French; law, legal; method, ways
fàn	饭	cooked rice; a meal; food
fāng	方	place, region; square shape; (a Chinese name)
fáng	房	house, building; a room
fàng	放	put, place; let go of; play (music); show (slides)
fēi	非	Africa; not, non-
fēi	飞	to fly

fēn	分	minute (of time); cent; to divide up
fěn	粉	powder
fēng	封	to seal, close up completely; (Measure for letters)
fēng	风	wind, breeze; customs, practice; scene, style
fú	服	clothing; to obey, yield to
fǔ	腐	to decay, to rot; corrupt; old, worn-out
fù	父	father

— G —

gāi	该	ought to, should
gān	干	dry; clean
gāng	刚	just now, just this moment
gǎng	港	harbor, port; (short for) Hong Kong
gāo	高	high, tall; (a Chinese family name)
gào	告	to tell, to inform; to accuse
gè	个	(general Measure)
gē	哥	elder brother
gěi	给	to give (to)
gēn	跟	together with; to follow
gèng/gēng	更	still more, even more / to change, alter
gōng	工	work, job; labor, laborer; engineering
gōng	公	public, open to all
gòng	共	common, same, collectively, all; to work together
gòu	够	enough, sufficient
guān	关	to close (up), to shut; relationship
guǎn	馆	hotel, restaurant; official residence or office
guàn	惯	accustomed to; habitual, customary

guì	贵	expensive
guó	国	country
guǒ	果	fruit; effect, result, consequence
guò	过	to pass, cross over; (particle of past experience)

— H —

hái	孩	child, children
hái	还	still, yet, also; or
hàn	汉	Chinese (people or language); Han (dynasty)
háng	行	a trade; a row of
hǎo	好	good, well; okay
hào	号	day (of month); number (of house); size (of clothing)
hē	喝	to drink
hé	和	and; peace, harmony
hěn	很	very
hóng	红	red (color)
hòu	后	rear of, back of; afterwards; descendants
hòu	候	period; to await
huā	花	to spend (money/time); flower
huà	话	(spoken) words, speech; language
huān	欢	joyful, glad, be pleased with
huán	还	to return (items borrowed)
huáng	黄	yellow (color) / (a Chinese family name)
huí	回	to return; to reply to; number of times/repetitions
huì	会	will, shall; can (i.e. know how to); an association
hūn	婚	marriage, wedding
huó	活	to live, to be alive; active, lively; movable, mobile

huǒ	火		fire
huò	或		or (used in statements), either; perhaps, may be

— J —

jī	机		machine; opportunity
jī	鸡		chicken
jí	级		grade or year (in school); degree or rank
jǐ	几		How many? a few, some
jǐ	己		self, oneself
jì	记		to remember; to recollect; to record (in writing)
jì	寄		to mail
jiā	加		to add (to), to increase
jiā	家		home; family; specialist
jià / jiǎ	假		vacation, holiday / false, not real; supposing if
jiān	间		the space between; (Measure for rooms)
jiǎn	简		simple, concise, succinct, brief
jiàn	件		(Measure for items, things, clothing)
jiàn	见		to meet; to see; to visit or call on; perceive (RVE)
jiāo / jiào	教		to teach / to educate; a religion
jiāo	蕉		banana
jiǎo / jiào	较		comparatively; to compare; to compete
jiào	叫		to be called (by a name); tell/order (someone)
jiào	觉		a sleep or a nap
jiē	街		street
jié	结		to unite, to connect; to tie, to knot; result, outcome
jié	节		festival, season
jiě	姐		elder sister; young lady

jiè	借	to lend/borrow
jīn	今	now, the present
jīn	斤	*jin* (500 gm.)
jìn	近	near (to), close (to) (in space and time)
jìn	进	to go ahead, advance, proceed; to improve
jīng	京	capital (of a country)
jīng	经	to pass through; classic books; to manage, to plan
jǐng	警	to warn, caution; to guard, keep watch
jiǔ	九	9
jiǔ	久	long (in time)
jiù	就	then, thereupon; only, just; right away
jù	具	utensil, tool, equipment
jú	局	office, bureau
jué	觉	to feel that; to realise that

K

kǎ	卡	a card; cardboard
kāi	开	to open (up); to leave (of trains and scheduled buses)
kàn / kān	看	to see; to visit; to read; to look at / keep an eye on
kǎo	考	to test or examine
kě	可	may, can; but, however; indeed, certainly
kè	客	guest, stranger; spectator; alien, non-native
kè	课	lesson
kòng / kōng	空	to have free/spare time / empty, vacant; sky or space
kǒu	口	mouth; oral; an opening; (Measure for people)
kuài	快	fast, quick; about to, soon; happy
kuài	块	dollar; a piece or lump (of)

— L —

lái	来	to come (to)
lǎo	老	old (in years), elderly
le	了	(suffix of change in situation *or* action completed)
lè	乐	happy, joyful, glad
lèi / lěi	累	tired, tiring, weary / to accumulate, pile up
lí	离	from (i.e. distance from); to leave, depart
lǐ	李	(a Chinese family name); plum
lǐ	里	in(side)
lǐ	礼	courtesy, polite; rites, ceremony; a gift or present
lián	连	to connect or join (up); even
liàn	练	to practice, train, exercise
liǎng	两	2 (must be followed by a Measure)
liàng	亮	bright, radiant, luminous
liǎo	了	(RVE indicating possibility, ability or completion)
lín	林	(a Chinese family name)
lìng	另	another, besides, in addition to
liú	刘	(a Chinese family name)
liù	六	6
lóu	楼	(number of the) floor (in a building); storied building
lù	路	road, path; way, route
lù	录	to record (sound); to take down (notes)
lǚ	旅	traveler, passenger; to travel; to lodge

— M —

ma	吗	(interrogative sentence particle)

mā	妈	mom
mǎ	马	horse; (a Chinese family name)
mǎi	买	to buy
mài	卖	to sell
màn	慢	slow, unhurried
máng	忙	busy, in haste, short of time
me	么	(interrogative particle)
méi	没	not
měi	每	each, every
měi	美	beautiful; America
mèi	妹	younger sister
men	们	(Noun suffix indicating the plural)
mén	门	door, gate
mǐ	米	(uncooked) rice; metre (linear measurement)
miàn	面	side, face; noodles, flour
míng	名	name; given name
míng	明	clear, bright
mǔ	母	mother; female

— N —

ná	拿	to take hold of or carry (smaller items)
nǎ	哪	Which?
nà	那	that
nǎi	奶	milk; grandma; breasts
nán	男	male (of humans)
nán	南	south
nán	难	difficult, hard (to do), unpleasant (to do)

ne	呢	(used in questions *or* to indicate ongoing action)
néng	能	can (in the sense of "be able to")
nǐ	你	you
nián	年	year
niàn	念	to read *aloud*; to study
niú	牛	cow, ox, cattle, bull
nǚ	女	female (of humans)

— P —

pái	排	a row or line (of); to expel, reject
pǎo	跑	to run; to flee
péng	朋	friend
piān / piàn	片	photograph / a piece or slice
pián	便	cheap
piào / piǎo	漂	pretty, attractive / to bleach / piāo: to float
piào	票	ticket

— Q —

qī	七	7
qī	期	a period of time
qí	骑	to ride (straddle)
qǐ	起	to arise, to get up; to rise
qì	汽	steam, gas, vapor
qì	气	air, gas, breath; anger
qiān	千	1,000
qián	前	front; previous, former

qián	钱	money
qiě	且	furthermore, moreover, still
qīn	亲	parents, relatives
qīng	青	green, blue, black; young, youth(ful)
qīng	清	clear, pure, clean; virtuous, honest; Qing (dynasty)
qíng	情	fact, detail; feeling, emotion; love, affection
qǐng	请	to ask/request to ...; to invite; please ...
qiú	球	a ball, a globe, ball-shaped
qù	去	to go (to)
qù	趣	interesting, funny; interest, fun

— R —

r	儿	Noun suffix
rán	然	nevertheless, but, although
rè	热	hot, to heat; earnest, zealous, enthusiastic
rén	人	man, person, people
rèn	认	to recognize; to admit; to resign oneself to
rì	日	day; sun; Japan
róng	容	easy; to contain or hold; face, expression
ròu	肉	meat, flesh
rú	如	if, supposing; as, be like

— S —

sān	三	3
sè	色	a color; sensuality, lust; appearance, looks
shān	山	mountain, hill

shāng	商	trade, commerce, business; to discuss, confer
shàng	上	on, up, above; ascend, get into; last (week/month)
shāo	烧	to burn; to roast (meat)
shǎo/shào	少	little (in quantity), few; less / young, youthful
shè	舍	an inn or house
shéi	谁	Who?
shén	什	What?
shēng	生	to be born; a literary person
shī	师	teacher, tutor, specialist
shí	十	10
shí	时	time; era, age
shí	识	to recognize, to know
shǐ	始	beginning, start
shì	市	market; city, municipality
shì	事	matter, item of business; job, task
shì	士	scholar, man of learning; soldier
shì	是	to be
shì	试	to test or examine; to have a try at
shòu	授	to teach, to tutor
shū	书	book
shū	舒	to relax; to unfold, stretch; slow, leisurely
shuǐ	水	water
shuì	睡	to sleep
shuō	说	to say, to speak; to say that
sī	司	to be in charge of
sī	思	to think, consider; to remember, recall
sì	四	4
sòng	送	give (gifts); send/deliver (goods); see off (guests)

sù	宿	to stay overnight, to lodge
sù	诉	to tell, to inform; to accuse, to file a complaint
suàn	算	to calculate, to compute; to plan (to)
suī	虽	although
suǒ	所	that which; place, location; building or office

— T —

tā	他	he, him
tā	她	she, her
tái	台	raised platform; (Meas. for electrical equip./machines)
tài	太	too, excessively
tán	谈	to chat, to converse, to talk over
tí	题	topic, subject (for discussion)
tiān	天	day; sky, heaven
tiáo	条	(Measure for long, narrow objects)
tīng	听	to listen to, to hear; to obey
tíng	停	to stop; to park (a vehicle)
tóu	头	the head; top, first, chief; (localizer suffix)

— W —

wài	外	outside; foreign
wán	完	to finish, to complete; whole, perfect
wán	玩	to play or amuse oneself (at or with)
wǎn	晚	evening; late
wǎn	碗	(rice) bowl, a bowl (of)
wàn	万	10,000

wáng	王	king; (a Chinese family name)
wǎng	往	to go towards (a given direction); in the past
wèi / wéi	为	for, on behalf of / to be; to do, to handle
wèi	位	(polite Measure for people)
wén	文	written language
wèn	问	to ask (a question), to inquire
wǒ	我	I, me
wú	吴	(a Chinese family name)
wǔ	五	5
wǔ	午	noon

— **X** —

xī	西	west
xī	息	to stop, to end; news, tidings
xí	习	to practice, learn; habit, custom
xǐ	洗	to wash
xǐ	喜	joyful, glad, be pleased with
xià	下	down, below; descend, go down; next (week/month)
xiān	先	first
xiān	鲜	fresh; bright, attractive
xiàn	现	now, at the present time
xiāng / xiàng	相	reciprocal, one another, mutual / facial features
xiāng	香	tasty, delicious; fragrant; incense, balm
xiǎng	想	to think (that/about), to think (of doing)
xiàng	向	to face towards (a given direction); until now
xiàng	像	such as; to be like, seem like, to resemble
xiǎo	小	small, little; young (in age)

xiào	校	school
xiē	些	a few, some; (the plural Measure)
xiě	写	to write
xiè	谢	to thank; (a Chinese family name)
xīn	心	the mind; the heart or core; intention, idea
xīn	新	new
xìn	信	letter (mail); to believe or trust (in)
xīng	星	star or planet
xíng	行	okay, alright; to walk; baggage
xìng / xīng	兴	cheerful, happy; interests / to prosper, to thrive
xìng	姓	to be surnamed, surname
xiū	休	to rest, to pause, to cease, to stop
xū	需	to need (to), needs
xǔ	许	perhaps, may be; permit, allow; (Chinese name)
xué	学	to study, learn, to learn how to

— Y —

yáng	杨	(a Chinese family name)
yàng	样	kind, variety (of); style, pattern; appearance, looks
yào	要	to want; want to, going to
yé	爷	grandfather; master, sir
yě	也	also, too
yī	一	1
yī	衣	clothing
yī	医	(medical) doctor, physician; to heal, treat diseases
yí	宜	right, proper
yǐ	已	already

yǐ	以	because of, by means of
yì	易	easy, lenient; Book of Changes
yì	意	meaning; intention; idea
yīn	因	because (of), for; cause, reason
yīn	音	sound, voice; a musical note; news/information
yín	银	silver; money, wealth
yìn	印	to print, imprint; a seal or chop, imprint, mark
yīng / yìng	应	ought to, should / to respond to; to deal with
yīng	英	English; British; handsome; outstanding
yǐng	影	shadow, image, reflection; to copy & imitate
yòng	用	to use; use (Noun); with, using
yóu	油	oil, fat, grease; inflammable liquid
yóu	邮	postal, mail
yǒu	友	friend, friendly
yǒu	有	there is/are; to have
yòu	又	again, also
yòu	右	right (side)
yú	鱼	fish
yǔ	语	spoken language
yuán	元	dollar; the beginning; Yuan (dynasty)
yuán	园	park, garden
yuǎn	远	far away, distant
yuàn	院	courtyard, yard; hall, court, college
yuàn	愿	be willing to, be desirous of; an aspiration
yuè	乐	music
yuè	月	month; moon
yùn	运	to transport (goods); to utilize; luck, fortune

Z

zài	再	again (future), more (i.e. additionally); still, further
zài	在	to be (located) at; in, at, on
zǎo	早	early; ago, before; Good Morning!
zěn	怎	How? Why? In what way? How is it that…?
zhàn	站	to stand; a (train) station, a (bus) stop
zhāng	张	(Measure for stamps & flat objects); (Chinese name)
zhǎng	长	to grow; senior, elder
zháo / zhāo	着	(RVE of successful attainment) / worried, anxious
zhǎo	找	to look for, "hunt" for
zhào	照	to shine upon; to care for; license, certificate
zhào	赵	(a Chinese family name)
zhe	着	(Verb suffix indicating continuing of action)
zhè	这	this
zhēn	真	really, truly; real, true
zhèng	正	in the middle of (doing something); exactly
zhī	知	to know
zhǐ / zhī	只	only, just / (Meas. for animals & birds; one of a pair)
zhǐ	纸	paper
zhōng	中	middle; China
zhōng	钟	o'clock; a clock; bells (which toll)
zhǒng / zhòng	种	kind or sort (of); seeds (of grains) / to plant, sow
zhòng	重	heavy, weighty; severe; important
zhōu	州	county (in old China); a state (in America)
zhū	猪	pig
zhù	住	to live, to reside
zhǔn	准	a standard or norm; accurate; to approve, to allow

zhuō	桌	table (for eating)
zi	子	(Noun suffix)
zì	字	word; written (Chinese) character
zì	自	self, oneself, personally; from
zǒu	走	to depart, to leave; to walk; to go (by way of)
zuì	最	the most, -est (= the superlative)
zuó	昨	yesterday
zuǒ	左	left (side)
zuò	作	to do, make, write, compose, act the part of
zuò	坐	to sit; to ride or go by (a conveyance with seats)
zuò	做	to do, to make, to engage in

CHINESE

CHARACTER

LIST

— A —

a	啊	(exclamatory particle)	4
ài	爱	love, affection; be fond (of)	3
ān	安	peaceful, quiet; to put/place	5

— B —

bá	拔	to uproot, to pull out (e.g. teeth)	5
bǎ	把	a handle/hold; to watch over	1
bān	般	kind (of), sort (of), class (of)	2
bì	币	currency, money	6
biān	鞭	to whip, flog; firecrackers	1
biàn	变	to change; uncommon; tragedy	2
bìng	并	and, also; even, equal with	3
bù	布	cloth, textiles	3

— C —

cāi	猜	to guess; to suspect	1
cān	参	to participate in; to visit	8
cǎo	草	grass, herb; draft (copy)	5
chǎn	产	to produce, to bring about; to bear (offspring)	9
chǎng	厂	factory, workshop	6
chàng	唱	to sing; to chant	2
chǎo	吵	to quarrel, to dispute; to disturb	6
chèn	趁	to take advantage of (an opportunity)	2
chéng	成	to become; to accomplish; 10%	2

chū	初	first; original; junior; early	10
chǔ	处	to deal with; to be faced with	2
chù	处	a place/location; a department	2
chuán	传	to propagate, pass on, spread	2
chuán	船	boat, ship	5
chuī	吹	to blow, puff; to brag, boast	2
cí	词	words, phrases, expressions	15
cǐ	此	this, these; such, thus	12
cōng	聪	clever, astute, bright	6
cūn	村	village, hamlet	10

— D —

dā / dá	答	to answer, reply; reciprocate	3
dāi	待	to stay (at a place); later on	4
dài	待	to treat (someone); await for	4
dài	代	be a substitute; generation, era	5
dàn	弹	a pellet	9
dǎo	倒	to be overthrown; to topple	1
dào	倒	to invert; on the contrary; to pour	1
dēng	灯	lamp, light, lantern	2
dī	低	to lower; low	3
dì	帝	imperial; emperor, ruler; a god	2
diào	掉	to drop, fall; to turn, move	4
dōng	冬	winter	1
dòng	洞	a cave, a hole; to see, penetrate	3
dú	读	to study; to read	1
dù	肚	stomach, abdomen, bowels	4

duān	端	an extreme; carry gingerly; proper; beginning	4
duàn	段	M: period of time; section, division; paragraph	10
dùn	顿	Measure for a meal; to pause	1
duǒ	朵	a flower; the lobe of the ear	11

— E —

ēn	恩	grace, favor, gratitude	5

— F —

fán	烦	annoy, trouble, worry, be vexed	6
fǎn	反	reverse, opposite; to turn back	4
fǎng	访	to visit, call on; inquire about	4
fén	坟	grave or mound	5
fū	夫	man, adult, male, master	3
fú	符	identification tag; a charm; to tally	15
fú	福	happiness, blessing, bliss	1
fù	附	near to; rely on; to enclose; add to	14
fù	复	complex; double; repeat; reply; recover	15

— G —

gǎi	改	to change, alter, modify	10
gài	盖	to cover; a lid; to build, construct; affix (a seal)	3
gài	概	general, overall, roughly	5
gǎn	感	to feel, perceive; feeling, emotion	3
gǎn	敢	to dare (to); bold, courageous	11

gǎn	赶	to hasten; to pursue; to expel	8
gàn	干	to do, to attend to some matter	7
gē	歌	a song; to sing, chant, praise	2
gè	各	each, every; all	2
gōng	功	effort; function; merit	7
gōng	恭	respectful, reverent	4
gǔ	古	ancient, antiquated	1
gǔ	骨	bone; framework, skeleton	15
gù	故	cause, reason; incident; former	1
gù	顾	to care for, look after; look at	7
guà	挂	to hang (up); be anxious; register	2
guài	怪	strange, queer; monster; to blame	3
guǎn	管	to take heed to; to manage; a tube	1
guì	跪	to kneel	5

— **H** —

hǎi	海	sea, ocean	13
hài	害	to harm, to injure, to damage	8
hán	寒	cold, chilly, wintry	5
hǎn	喊	to shout, to cry out, to scream	10
hé	河	river, waterway	8
hēi	黑	dark; black (color); sinister	2
hù	户	household, family; a door	1
huá	划	to row (a boat); an oar	8
huà	化	to convert, transform; chemistry	2
huà	画	paint, draw; to design; to mark off	2
huài	坏	bad; broken down; vicious	7

huàn	换	to change; to exchange	8
huáng	皇	imperial, royal	2
huò	获	to get, obtain, reap, capture	12

— **J** —

jí	急	urgent, hurried; anxious	9
jì	季	season; quarter(ly)	5
jì	纪	historical record; age; a century	4
jì	计	to calculate; a scheme, plot; a plan	5
jì	继	to continue; to inherit, succeed to	2
jiǎ	甲	armor, shell, crust; 1st of the 10 Celestial Stems	15
jiān	煎	to fry (in shallow fat or oil)	6
jiàn	健	healthy, strong; vigorous; capable	9
jiǎng	讲	to talk, speak; to explain; to be fussy about	7
jiāo	交	to intersect; to exchange; hand in	1
jiǎo	脚	foot; leg or base (of something)	2
jiǎo	饺	stuffed dumpling	6
jiē	接	to receive; to welcome; to connect	1
jiě	解	to explain; to solve; to understand; to untie	11
jiè	介	to lie between; upright	3
jiè	界	to demarcate; domain, territory	6
jīn	金	gold; metal; money, wealth	2
jǐn	紧	tight, firm; urgent, pressing	9
jīng	睛	the eye-ball, the pupil of the eye	2
jǐng	景	scenery, view; circumstances	5
jìng	净	clean, pure; to cleanse, purify; vain	1
jìng	静	quiet & peaceful; motionless	5

jiū	究	to examine, investigate; finally	4
jiǔ	酒	wine, liquor, alcoholic drink	1
jiù	救	to save, to deliver, to rescue	12
jú	菊	chrysanthemum	14
jù	句	a sentence	1
jù	聚	to assemble, gather (together)	1
jué	决	to decide; certain, sure	3
jué	诀	knack; sorcery; to part, separate	13

— K —

kāng	康	healthy	9
kē	棵	(Measure for trees)	15
kè	刻	to engrave; quarter-hour; cruel	15
kǒng	孔	(family name) / a hole/opening	9
kū	哭	to cry, weep, wail	3
kǔ	苦	bitter; miserable, difficult	1
kùn	困	difficult; poor; weary, fatigued	9

— L —

lā	拉	to pull, drag; lengthen, elongate	5
láng	郎	husband, man; master	3
lāo	捞	to pull or drag out of the water	6
lěng	冷	cold (lit. & fig.)	2
lǐ	理	reason, cause; law, principle	1
lì	力	strength, power; vigorously	5
lì	莉	white jasmine	4

lì	历	to pass through, to undergo; an era, an age	2
lì	丽	beautiful, fine, elegant	2
liǎ	俩	the two; a couple	9
lián	联	to unite, to connect, to join	1
liǎn	脸	face (lit. & fig.)	3
liáng	凉	cool, chilly	14
liáo	聊	to chat	2
lìng	令	to cause something to happen	1
liú	流	to flow, wander; a division, rank	6
lóng	龙	dragon; imperial, of the emperor	2
lóng	笼	a bamboo cage; to encompass	2
lǜ	绿	green (color)	4
luò	落	to fall, descend; to decline, wither	4

— M —

má	麻	numb; hemp; pock-marked	6
máo	毛	(body) hair; woolen; dime	9
mào	貌	facial appearance; manner	9
mí	谜	riddle, conundrum, puzzle	2
mì	秘	secret, confidential; mysterious	13
miào	庙	temple, shrine	2
mín	民	the people	2
mò	茉	white jasmine	4
mù	木	wood; stupid, dumb-witted	5
mù	目	the eye; to look, to see; category	2
mù	墓	a grave, a tomb	5

— N —

nào	闹	to disturb, to agitate; noisy	2
niáng	娘	mother; girls or women	3
nóng	农	farming, agricultural	2
nǔ	努	to exert (effort)	5
nuǎn	暖	warm	2

— P —

pá	爬	to crawl, lie face down; to climb	2
pà	怕	fear (that), be afraid of; perhaps	7
pāi	拍	to pat, to slap; music beat	8
pào	炮	a cannon, big gun	1
pí	皮	skin, fur, leather, rind; naughty	6
píng	平	equality; level, even; peaceful	2
pō	泼	to pour, to sprinkle	8

— Q —

qī	戚	relatives by marriage	1
qī	妻	wife	3
qí	其	this, that, the; he, she, it, they	2
qí	奇	strange, uncanny; wonderful	3
qí	棋	chess	9
qiáng	强	strong, powerful, vigorous	7
qiǎo	巧	ingenious, skillful; a clever feat; coincidence	15
qiè / qiē	切	be close to / to slice, carve, cut	8
qín	琴	a stringed musical instrument	9

qīng	轻	light (weight); simple, easy; mild	2
qiū	秋	autumn	5
qiú	求	to plead for, beg for, pray for	11
qū	屈	(Chinese name); humiliate; to bend	10
qǔ	娶	(of a man) to take a wife	11
quán	全	whole, complete; perfect; absolute	1
què	却	however, but, still, yet	6

— R —

ràng	让	to let; to allow; by; to yield	2
rēng	扔	to throw, to hurl; to abandon, to discard	8
réng	仍	still, yet	1

— S —

sài	赛	to compete, contest, tournament	8
sǎo	扫	to sweep; exterminate; weed out	1
sào	扫	broom	1
shā	杀	to kill, put to death, slaughter	8
shǎng	赏	to appreciate; to bestow, to grant	12
shào	绍	bring together, join; continue	3
shè	社	society, community, organization	3
shēn	身	the body; in person, oneself	4
shēn	深	deep (water/thoughts); dark (color)	8
shén	神	god, divine, supernatural	12
shēng	声	voice, sound; fame, make known	8
shéng	绳	rope, cord; to rectify, to correct	15

shèng	剩	to be left over, residue, in excess	12
shī	诗	poem; poetry	4
shī	失	to lose; to neglect, let slip; an omission, mistake	5
shí	拾	to pick up, collect; 10 (official)	1
shí	食	food; to eat	4
shí	实	real, true; practical; tangible	4
shǐ	史	history, chronicles, annals	4
shǐ	使	to make, act; to use, employ	5
shì	世	world; generation	4
shì	示	to show, indicate, demonstrate	8
shì	式	model, style, mode, pattern	3
shì	视	to regard as; to look at, to see	11
shōu	收	to gather; to retrieve; to accept	1
shǒu	手	hand; a skilled person	2
shǒu	首	M: songs & poems; the first, beginning; leader	14
shòu	寿	longevity, old age; the life span	13
shòu	受	to receive; to endure, suffer	4
shú	熟	very familiar; (of fruit) ripe; (of food) cooked	15
shù / shǔ	数	number; several / to count	8
shù	树	tree; to erect, establish	4
shù	术	a skill, a feat; way or method	15
shuāng	双	a pair (of), a couple (of); both	3
shùn	顺	submit to, obey; smooth-going	7
sǐ	死	to die; extremely (= RVE)	4
sì	寺	temple, monastery, mosque	2
sú	俗	customs; common; vulgar	3
suí	随	to submit to; to accompany	3
suì	岁	a year; age (of a person)	1

— T —

tā	它	it (neuter gender)	1
tán	弹	to play (a stringed instrument); to rebound	9
táng	堂	hall; relatives of the same grandfather	7
tè	特	special, unique, unusual	2
téng	疼	to ache, be painful; be fond of	11
tí	提	mention; lift by hand; to obtain	2
tǐ	体	the body; shape, form	4
tián	田	(rice) fields, cultivated land	7
tiào	跳	jump, leap; throb; skip over, omit	2
tiē	贴	to paste on; to subsidize; appropriate	1
tíng	庭	a hall or yard; court of justice	1
tōng	通	to communicate; to lead to	1
tóng	同	same; together; equal; to agree	1
tǒng	统	to unify, unite; totally; to govern	5
tòng	痛	pain, aching; sorrowful, sad, bitter; heartily	12
tū	突	sudden; to jut out; a break through	12
tú	图	chart, diagram; conspire, scheme	2
tǔ	土	earth, soil; native; land, ground	8
tù	兔	rabbit, hare	12

— W —

wáng	亡	dead; to perish; to flee	14
wàng	忘	to forget; to neglect, overlook	1
wàng	望	hope, expect; to view, watch	1
wéi	围	to encircle, surround, hem in	9

wěi	伟	extraordinary, great; gigantic	9
wèi	味	flavor, taste, smell, odor	4
wū	屋	room; house	1
wǔ	舞	to dance; to brandish; stir up, agitate	2
wù	物	thing, matter; the physical world	1

— X —

xī	悉	to know; all, total, entire	15
xī	希	hope, desire, long for; strange	1
xī	夕	dusk, evening; slanting, oblique	1
xì	系	relationship; department; system	15
xì	细	detailed; slender; fine, intricate	4
xià	夏	summer; a Chinese dynasty	4
xiàn	线	thread, wire; a line	5
xiàn	馅	stuffing, filling (for dumplings)	6
xiǎng	响	to sound, to ring; a sound, echo	10
xiàng	象	a portrait; elephant, ivory	3
xiāo	宵	night, dark, evening	2
xiāo	消	to disappear, die out; to disperse, eliminate	5
xiào	孝	be filial to one's parents	7
xiào	笑	to laugh, smile; to ridicule, deride	1
xīn	辛	hard, toilsome; bitter, acrid	1
xīn	欣	glad(ly), joyful(ly), delighted	14
xìng	幸	well-being, happy; luckily	3
xiōng	兄	elder brother; term of respect	13
xū	须	to have to; necessary; a beard	1
xù	续	to continue, renew, extend	2

xuě	雪	snow	14

— Y —

yā	鸭	duck	1
yán	研	to investigate, to research	4
yán	颜	dyes, colors; features; reputation	1
yǎn	眼	the eye; tiny hole or opening	2
yàn	验	to test, examine; verify, prove	3
yáng	阳	sun; male, masculine; positive	2
yào	药	medicine, medicinal drugs	4
yè	叶	leaf, petal	4
yè	夜	night, dark	1
yì	义	righteousness, justice; generosity; meaning	14
yì	艺	art, skill, talent	15
yīn	姻	(relations through) marriage	3
yíng	迎	to receive; to greet, welcome	1
yìng	硬	hard, stiff; inflexible, rigid	6
yǒng	永	eternal, everlasting, permanent	3
yóu	尤	especially; mistake; feel bitter	2
yóu	由	by, up to; from; reason, cause	3
yú	于	then, than; in, on, at, by, from	4
yǔ	雨	rain	5
yù	育	to educate; to raise; give birth to	9
yù	遇	to encounter; to treat; opportunity	9
yuán	原	origin, source, beginning	1
yuán	圆	round; complete; satisfactory	2
yuè	越	the more; to cross over	5

— Z —

zá	杂	miscellaneous; to mix, to blend	15
zāng	脏	dirty, filthy	8
zǎo	澡	to wash, to bathe	8
zhāng	章	chapter	1
zhàng	丈	an elder, a senior	3
zhāo	招	to beckon (with the hand); to recruit; to attract	4
zhě	者	(particle used to form adverbials)	3
zhēng	筝	kite; kind of stringed instrument	5
zhěng	整	entire; exactly; orderly; to tidy up	1
zhèng	挣	to earn (money / a living)	1
zhī	之	of (= possessive particle)	10
zhí	直	straight; direct; continuous; frank	2
zhōng	终	conclusion; finally; to pass away	15
zhōu	舟	boat, ship	10
zhǔ	煮	to boil, to stew; to cook (meals)	6
zhǔ	主	lord, master, chief; officiate at	3
zhù	助	to assist, to help, to aid	2
zhù	注	to direct one's gaze; pour (liquids)	3
zhù	祝	to wish; celebrate; congratulate	1
zhuàn	传	biography	2
zhuāng	装	to install, pack, load; to store, to keep; to pretend	1
zǒng	总	always; chief; all, overall, general	13
zòng	粽	glutinous rice tamale	10
zú	族	tribe, clan; family/class (of)	8
zǔ	祖	ancestor; founder, originator	5

活到老
学到老

CHINESE - ENGLISH VOCABULARY LIST

— A —

àiguó	爱国	(SV)	patriotic	10
àiqíng	爱情	(BF)	love (between man & woman)	9
àishàng	爱上	(RV)	to love	8

— B —

bá	拔	(V)	to uproot, to pull out (e.g. teeth)	5
bái tù	白兔	(N)	white rabbit (M: 只)	12
bài(bai)	拜(拜)	(V)	to worship	12
bàifǎng	拜访	(V)	to visit, pay a call on	4
bǐrú (shuō)	比如(说)	(EX)	for example	1
biānpào	鞭炮	(N)	string of firecrackers	1
biǎomiàn	表面	(N)	on the surface	15
biǎoshì	表示	(V)	to show, indicate, express	8
biǎoxiàn	表现	(N)	a show of (what one means)	5
biǎoxiàn	表现	(V)	to behave (in a certain way)	5
bǔ shēntǐ	补身体	(VO)	to nourish one's body	11
bù	布	(N)	cloth (M: 块 piece of)	3

— C —

cáinéng	才能	(N)	talent, abilities	10
cǎodì	草地	(N)	grass meadow, pasture	5
chǎnshēng	产生	(V)	to produce, to give rise to	9

chángjiǔ	长久	(TW)	a very long time	14
chángshòu	长寿	(N)	longevity, a long life	13
chéng jiā	成家	(VO)	to get married	10
chéngyǔ	成语	(N)	4-character idiom or saying	15
chéngzhǎng	成长	(V/N)	grow (in maturity) / growth	9
chī hē wán lè	吃喝玩乐	(PH)	to eat, drink and be merry	12
Chóngyángjié	重阳节	(N)	Double Ninth Festival	14
chū	初		first; original; junior; early	10
chū wèntí	出问题	(VO)	to incur problems	3
chūxiàn	出现	(V)	to appear, to emerge	5
chū zhǔyi	出主意	(VO)	to provide an idea, give advice	3
chúdiào	除掉	(V)	to remove, get rid of (obstacles)	8
chúxī	除夕	(N)	Lunar New Year's Eve	1
Chǔ guó	楚国	(PW)	the Country of Chu	10
chǔlǐ	处理	(V)	deal with, sort out (problems)	9
chuánshuō	传说	(V/N)	rumor has it / legends, hearsay	2
chuántǒng	传统	(N/SV)	tradition / traditional	5
chuī	吹	(V)	to blow, puff	2
chūnlián	春联	(N)	New Year couplets	1
cóng cǐ yǐhòu	从此以后		from this time on, from now on	12
cóngqián	从前	(A)	formerly, in the past	1

— D —

dǎ-jié	打结	(VO)	to tie a knot	15
dǎ lái dǎ qù	打来打去	(PH)	to fight back & forth	10

dàduōshù	大多数	(N)	the majority (of)	8
dàfang	大方	(SV)	generous & liberal	4
dàhuì	大会	(N)	conference, large meeting	14
dàmǐ	大米	(N)	white rice or pearl rice	6
dài	代	(M)	generation	7
dàibiǎo	代表	(V/N)	to represent / representative	5
dāngzhōng	当中	(PW)	in the middle (of)	10
dāng...de shíhou	当……的时候		when	7
dào	倒	(V)	to invert, place upside down	1
dàolǐ	道理	(N)	teaching; right or proper way	9
dēngjié	灯节	(N)	Lantern Festival	2
dēnglong	灯笼	(N)	a lantern	2
děng dào	等到	(V)	by the time when, until	7
dìshang	地上	(PW)	on the ground	2
dìwèi	地位	(N)	social position or standing	3
diǎn	点	(M)	a point (e.g. in a lecture)	8
dōngnánbù	东南部	(PW)	south-east region/area	5
dúshūrén	读书人	(N)	a person of learning, a scholar	15
dúyīn	读音	(N)	pronunciation (of a word)	14
duìbuqǐ	对不起	(V)	to let (someone) down badly	7
duìfāng	对方	(N)	the opposite party, other side	3
duìxiàng	对象	(N)	(marriage) partner	3
duìzhe	对着	(V)	facing (an object or person)	4
duōme	多么	(A)	How...! What a ...!	4

— E —

| ér | 而 | (Con) | but, and yet, nevertheless | 4 |

— F —

fāmíng	发明	(V/N)	to invent / an invention	6
fǎn'ér	反而	(A)	on the contrary	8
fāngshì	方式	(N)	approach, method	3
féndì	坟地	(N)	graveyard, cemetery	5
fénmù	坟墓	(N)	a grave	5
fēngzheng	风筝	(N)	kite	5
fūqī	夫妻	(N)	married couple; husband & wife	3
fúhào	符号	(N)	a symbol, a sign	15
fúqì	福气	(N)	blessing, good luck	7

— G —

gǎibiàn	改变	(V/N)	change, alter / transformation	10
gǎn	赶	(V)	to drive (out/away), to expel	10
gǎn'ēn	感恩	(VO)	to be thankful for	5
gǎn'ēnjié	感恩节	(N)	Thanksgiving Day	5
gǎnqíng	感情	(N)	emotional feelings	4
gàn (huór)	干(活儿)	(VO)	to work, to do a job	7
gēshēng	歌声	(N)	the sound of singing	8
gèzhǒnggèyàng	各种各样		each & every kind of	2

gèzi	个子	(N)	physical size of a person, build	11
gōnggòng	公共	(BF)	public (relations, health, etc.)	9
gǔ	古	(SV)	ancient, antiquated	1
gǔdài	古代	(TW)	ancient times	9
gǔlǎo	古老	(SV)	ancient, antiquated	8
gǔwén	古文	(N)	ancient style of Chinese writing	15
gǔtou	骨头	(N)	bone	15
gùyì	故意	(A)	intentionally, on purpose	1
guǎn	管	(V)	to pay heed to, pay attention to	13
guì	跪	(V)	to kneel	5
guómín	国民	(N)	citizen, the people	2
guówáng	国王	(N)	king, monarch	10

— H —

hàipà	害怕	(SV)	fearful, to be scared/afraid of	8
Hánshíjié	寒食节	(N)	Cold Food Festival	5
hǎn	喊	(V)	to shout, to cry out, to scream	10
Hànrén	汉人	(N)	the Han Chinese	8
Hànzú	汉族	(N)	the Han Chinese (ethnic group)	8
hǎohuà	好话	(N)	a good word, word of praise	3
hé ... yǒu guān	和……有关		related to ..., connected with ...	11
hépíng	和平	(N/SV)	peace / peaceful (living)	9
hěn jiǔ yǐ lái	很久以来	(PH)	for a long time now	11
hóngbāo	红包	(N)	a red envelope containing money	1
hóngniáng	红娘	(N)	matchmaker	3

hòudài	后代	(N)	descendants	10
huángdì	皇帝	(N)	emperor	2
hūnyīn	婚姻	(N)	marriage	3

— J —

jìhào	记号	(N)	a mark, a sign	15
jìniàn	纪念	(V/N)	to commemorate / remembrance	4
jìsuàn	计算	(V)	to calculate	5
jiājiāhùhù	家家户户	(N)	every family and household	1
jiāwù	家务	(N)	domestic chores, housework	7
jiǎgǔwén	甲骨文	(N)	oracle bone writings	15
jiàn(dào)	见(到)	(V)	to see	7
jiāohuì	教会	(RV)	to teach until mastered	9
jiē	接	(V)	follow on after another	7
jiēshòu	接受	(V)	to accept	5
jiēzhe	接着	(A)	thereupon, shortly afterwards	7
jiéqì	节气	(N)	24 seasonal periods in a year	5
jièkǒu	借口	(N)	an excuse	10
jīnlóng	金龙	(N)	golden dragon	2
jǐn	紧	(SV/A)	tight, taut / tightly	11
jiǔ bēi	酒杯	(N)	wine glass, wine cup	4
jiù	救	(V)	to save, to deliver, to rescue	12
júhuā	菊花	(N)	chrysanthemum (flower)	14

— K —

kànshàng	看上	(RV)	to take a fancy to	2
kànzhòng	看重	(V)	to regard as important	7
kějiàn	可见		it's obvious/perceived that	4
kè	刻	(V)	to carve, engrave	15
kǒu	口	(M)	mouthful	4
kǒushuǐ	口水	(N)	saliva	6

— L —

láiwǎng	来往	(N)	social intercourse	8
lāo	捞	(V)	to pull or drag out of the water	6
lǎobǎixìng	老百姓	(N)	the (common) people	12
lǐmào	礼貌	(N)	good manners, politeness	9
lǐjiě	理解	(V)	to understand, to comprehend	11
lǐyóu	理由	(N)	reasons, grounds, explanations	4
lìqi	力气	(N)	physical strength	9
liǎ	俩	(NU)	the two	9
lìng rén	令人	(VO)	to make one (e.g. sad, angry)	1
liú kǒushuǐ	流口水	(VO)	to make one's mouth water	6
luò	落	(V)	to fall, descend; decline, wither	4

— M —

mànmanlái	慢慢来	(PH)	to take one's time, not rush	4
máobǐ	毛笔	(N)	Chinese writing brush	9

měihǎo	美好	(SV)	(of abstract things) happy, bright	1
mén	门	(M)	(Measure for courses/subjects)	4
mìjué	秘诀	(N)	the secret (e.g. of success)	13
miànfěn	面粉	(N)	flour	6
miànqián	面前	(PW)	in (someone's) presence, before	10
miànshí	面食	(N)	wheat foods (e.g. noodles)	4
mínsú	民俗	(N)	customs & practices of a people	8
mínzú	民族	(N)	an ethnic group; a nation	8
míngliàng	明亮	(SV)	bright, well illuminated	2
mòlìhuā	茉莉花	(N)	white jasmine (flower)	4

— N —

nánfāng	男方	(N)	the bridegroom's family	3
nánnǚpíngděng	男女平等	(PH)	equality of the sexes	11
nántīng	难听	(SV)	unpleasant to listen to, to grate	13
nào dòngfáng	闹洞房	(VO)	to disturb the bridal chamber	3
nénglì	能力	(N)	ability, capability	9
niánlǎo	年老	(SV)	aged	7
niányèfàn	年夜饭	(N)	dinner on Chinese New Year's Eve	1
niánzhǎng	年长	(SV)	older in age, senior	14
nónglì	农历	(N)	the lunar calendar	2
nǚfāng	女方	(N)	the bride's family	3
nǚshén	女神	(N)	goddess	12

— P —

pá	爬	(V)	to crawl, creep, lie face down	2
pāi-shǒu	拍手	(VO)	to clap (with the hands)	8
píng	平	(SV)	flat, even (surface)	15
Pōshuǐjié	泼水节	(N)	Water Splashing Festival	8

— Q —

qízhōng	其中	(N)	of which, of those/them	6
qǐ míngzi	起名字	(VO)	to name, to give a name to …	13
qiánhòu	前后	(TW)	or thereabouts (re. time)	5
qīnrén	亲人	(N)	close relatives	4
qǔ	娶	(V)	(of a man) to take a wife	11
què	却	(A)	however, but	6

— R —

ràng	让	(V)	give way to, yield, back down	10
rè'ài	热爱	(V/N)	love fervently / passionate love	9
rénjiā	人家	(N)	a home, residence; other people	2
rénmín	人民	(N)	the people	8
rénshēng	人生	(N)	(meaning of) life	5
rènshi zì	认识字	(VO)	to be literate, be able to read	9
réngrán	仍然	(A)	still, yet	1

— S —

sāndàitóngtáng	三代同堂	(PH)	3 generations under one roof	7
sǎo-mù	扫墓	(VO)	pay respects to one's ancestors	5
shāsǐ	杀死	(RV)	to kill, to murder	8
shǎng-yuè	赏月	(VO)	to enjoy the moonlight	12
shàng-xué	上学	(VO)	to go to school	2
shāo	烧	(V)	to boil, cook, roast, burn	4
shāokāi	烧开	(RV)	(of water) to bring to the boil	6
shǎoshù	少数	(N)	a minority	8
shǎoshùmínzú	少数民族	(N)	minority people group	8
shénqí	神奇	(SV)	wondrous, mysterious	12
shēngzhǎng	生长	(V/N)	to grow, to develop / growth	4
shéngzi	绳子	(N)	rope	15
shèngxia	剩下	(V)	to be left over, remainder	12
shīqù	失去	(V)	to lose ...	9
shīrén	诗人	(N)	poet	4
shídài	时代	(N)	age, era	11
shífēn	十分	(A)	100%, very, completely	1
shìshang	世上	(PW)	on the earth, in the world	5
shōuhuò	收获	(V/N)	to reap / harvest; fruit of effort	12
shōushi	收拾	(V)	to tidy up, put (things) in order	1
shōuxià	收下	(RV)	to accept, receive	3
shòu huānyíng	受欢迎	(VO)	to be well-received/liked	4
shòu jiàoyù	受教育	(VO)	to receive an education	9
shùmù	树木	(N)	trees	5

shùyè	树叶	(N)	tree leaf, foliage	4
shùzì	数字	(N)	numeral, figure, digit	14
shuāng fāng	双方	(N)	both parties, both sides	3
shuǐmiànshang	水面上	(PW)	on the surface of the water	6
shuōbudìng	说不定	(EX)	maybe, who can say, perhaps	8
shuōfǎ	说法	(N)	a way of reasoning	4
sīkǎo	思考	(V)	to think deeply about, ponder	5
sīxiǎng	思想	(V/N)	to think about / thoughts, ideas	9
sǐwáng	死亡	(N/V)	death / to die	14
sòng-zhōng	送终	(VO)	to prepare for a burial	15

— T —

tán-qín	弹琴	(VO)	to play a stringed instrument	9
tèdiǎn	特点	(N)	special features/characteristics	9
tèyǒude	特有的	(SV)	unique (to), special, exclusive to	8
tí	提	(V)	to mention; raise, lift by hand	2
tímù	题目	(N)	topic, subject	2
tiānkōng	天空	(PW)	the skies	5
tiānshang	天上	(PW)	in the heavens/skies	2
tiáojiàn	条件	(N)	conditions, terms (agreement)	1
tīng	听	(V)	to obey, be obedient to	7
tóngshí	同时	(A)	at the same time, simultaneously	1
tóngyàng	同样	(A)	alike, similar	13
tóngyīn	同音	(N)	the same tone, a homophone	15
tòngkǔ	痛苦	(SV/N)	to be painful; suffering, anguish	12

tūrán	突然	(A)	suddenly, unexpectedly	12
tú	图	(N)	picture, chart, diagram, map	2
túhuà	图画	(N)	picture, drawing	2
tùzi	兔子	(N)	rabbit, hare	12

— W —

wàidì	外地	(PW)	other parts of the country	1
wánchéng	完成	(V)	to complete, to accomplish	9
wǎn huì	晚会	(N)	evening gathering/party	8
wéiqí	围棋	(N)	"Encirclement Chess"	9
wěidà	伟大	(SV)	great, extraordinary	9
wénhuà	文化	(N)	culture, civilization	2
wénzì	文字	(N)	written language	15

— X —

xísú	习俗	(N)	custom, practice	11
xǐhuānshàng	喜欢上	(RV)	to like, have taken a fancy for	8
xǐjiǔ	喜酒	(N)	wedding feast	3
xǐshì	喜事	(N)	a happy occasion	3
xǐ-tóu	洗头	(VO)	to wash (one's) hair	11
xìxīn	细心	(SV)	careful, think of all aspects	4
xià jiǎozi	下饺子	(VO)	to place the *jiaozi* in the water	6
xià-shān	下山	(VO)	(of the sun) to set	2
xiàn	馅	(N)	stuffing, filling (for dumplings)	6

Chinese-English Vocabulary List 209

xiàndài	现代	(BF)	modern, contemporary	11
xiàndàihuà	现代化	(SV)	modern	11
xiāng'ài	相爱	(V)	to love one another	3
xiāngwèi(r)	香味(儿)	(N)	fragrant smell; aromatic flavor	4
xiǎng bànfǎ	想办法	(VO)	to think of a way/solution	9
xiǎngniàn	想念	(V)	to think affectionately of, miss	5
xiǎngxiàng	想象	(V)	to imagine, to suppose that	9
xiǎngxiànglì	想象力	(N)	(power of) imagination	9
xiāoshī	消失	(V)	to disappear, die out, vanish	5
xiàoshùn	孝顺	(V/SV)	to be filial to one's parents	7
xīnláng	新郎	(N)	bridegroom	3
xīnniáng	新娘	(N)	bride	3
xīnshēng'ér	新生儿	(N)	newborn child	13
xīnmù(zhōng)	心目(中)	(PW)	(in) one's heart or mind	7
xīnqíng	心情	(N)	mood (lit.: heart-feelings)	3
xīnshì	心事	(N)	matters/worries on the mind	4
xīnyì	心意	(N)	(heartfelt) idea or intention	5
xīnshǎng	欣赏	(V)	to enjoy, appreciate (a view)	14
xīngxing	星星	(N)	stars	12
xìngfú	幸福	(SV/N)	blissful / happiness & well-being	3
xuéwen	学问	(N)	erudition, learning, scholarship	4

— Y —

yàoshi	要是	(A)	if	6
yèzi	叶子	(N)	leaf	4

yíxiàzi	一下子	(N)	a moment, a short time space	6
yǐlái	以来		since (a point of time)	12
yìshēng	一生	(N)	whole life, a lifetime	13
yìshù	艺术	(N)	art	15
yíngjiē	迎接	(V)	to receive; to greet, welcome	1
yìngbì	硬币	(N)	coins	6
yǒngyuǎn	永远	(A)	eternally, forever	3
yòngchu	用处	(N)	use or purpose	14
yòng-lì	用力	(VO)	exert oneself, put forth strength	9
yòngxīn	用心	(SV)	(do sthg.) attentively or intently	9
yóu	油	(N)	oil	6
yǒu dàolǐ	有道理	(SV)	reasonable, plausible	9
yǒu fú(qì)	有福(气)	(SV)	blessed or favored by fortune	3
yǒu lǐmào	有礼貌	(SV)	courteous, well mannered	9
yǒu yìyì	有意义	(SV)	meaningful, significant	14
yǒu yòng	有用	(SV)	useful; beneficial	9
yuèyuán	月圆	(N)	full moon	2

— Z —

zhǎo máfan	找麻烦	(VO)	pick on somebody, find fault	7
zhào	照	(V)	to shine upon, illuminate	2
zhēnzhèng(de)	真正(的)	(A)	actual(ly), real(ly); genuine	3
zhěngzhěng	整整	(A)	whole, full, entire	11
zhī yī	之一		one of ...	10
zhǐqián	纸钱	(N)	paper money (for the dead)	5

zhōng	钟	(N)	a clock	15
zhōngjiān	中间	(PW)	(in) the middle/center	15
zhōng yào	中药	(N)	Chinese herbal medicine	11
zhòngdà	重大	(SV)	major, significant, important	7
zhòngnánqīngnǚ	重男轻女	(PH)	to regard males more highly	13
zhòngshì	重视	(SV)	to regard as important	11
zhǔrén	主人	(N)	host(ess) [polite]; master, lord	6
zhǔyào(de)	主要(的)	(SV)	major, essential, chief	4
zhù(fú)	祝(福)	(V)	to wish (as a blessing)	1
zhùfú	祝福	(N)	a blessing	1
zìyīn	字音	(N)	pronunciation of a character	15
zǔfù	祖父	(N)	grandfather	7
zǔfùmǔ	祖父母	(N)	grandparents	7
zǔmǔ	祖母	(N)	grandmother	7
zǔxiān	祖先	(N)	(one's) ancestors, forefathers	5
zuò-rén	做人	(VO)	conduct oneself appropriately	9
zuò-shì	做事	(VO)	do work of a casual nature	7
zuòyòng	作用	(N)	(drugs) effect; (machinery) uses	4
zuò yuèzi	坐月子	(VO)	confined to home for one month	11